PARENTS!
LOOSE YOUR CHILDREN *from* BONDAGE

(Enhanced Edition)

By
Abolaji Muyiwa Akinbo

Forward by D. K. Olukoya
(Mountain Of Fire and Miracles Ministries)

Copyright © 2015 by Abolaji Muyiwa Akinbo

Parents! Loose Your Children From Bondage (Enhanced Edition)
Forwarded by Dr D.K. Olukoya
by Abolaji Muyiwa Akinbo

Printed in the United States of America

ISBN 9781498425551

All rights reserved solely by the author. The author guarantees all contents are original and do not infringe upon the legal rights of any other person or work. No part of this book may be reproduced in any form without the permission of the author. The views expressed in this book are not necessarily those of the publisher.

Unless otherwise indicated, Scripture quotations are taken from the King James Version (KJV) – public domain.

www.xulonpress.com

Important Resources by Abolaji Muyiwa Akinbo:

Parent! Loose Your Children From Bondage

Created To Manifest!!!

Prayer, Power & Results!

Soy Creado Para Manifestarme!!!

PADRES! DESATEN SUS HIJOS DE ATADURAS

LA ORACIÓN, EL PODER Y LOS RESULTADOS!

FOREWORD

Children are the heritage of the Lord. They are the foundations of tomorrow's generation. The Bible says, "If the foundation be destroyed, what can the righteous do?"

The Church of GOD has, for a long time, closed her eyes on the issue of Children's Deliverance. The devil is fighting with wicked determination to pollute and destroy Children. It is sad, but it is true that even Children of dedicated Christians are among victims of satanic cages. Unfortunately, many parents are completely ignorant of the fact that Children are targets of the devil and that the host of hell knows that once you get the child, you got the man or woman.

The issue of troubled or attacked children is fast becoming a common affair. Is there a way out of this terrible situation? The good news is that there is a way out. Parents can cooperate with GOD to set their Children free from the evil grip of the enemy. Parents can learn the principles of forming spiritual barricades around their children.

This book by Pastor Akinbo is a spiritual hospital manual to enable Parents to cooperate with GOD to set their children free. I whole-heartedly recommend it for all serious Christian Parents. I pray that each word in this book will be a blessing to all its readers. (Amen.)

Dr. D. K. Olukoya
(General Overseer Mountain Of Fire and Miracles)

ACKNOWLEDGEMENT

I am heavily indebted to some special people who GOD used to make this book a huge success. Without them, this enhanced edition would have been impossible.

My prayer for them is that GOD will continue to renew their strength, the oil of GOD in their spiritual lamp will never dry and they will surely achieve their dreams and fulfill their potentials in JESUS' name.

Thank you Doranda Akinbo for all your support and help, you are the best wife a man can have. Thank you Ore, Ayo, and Sade for allowing daddy to work countless hours at home and always coming to check on me to make sure I am okay. Thank you Denise Abreu Quintana for type setting from the original book so that I can work on this edition, your talent is stunning. You are a true daughter. Thank you Anne Lunsford for your immeasurable support you will never understand how much difference you make. Thank you Mike Granam for redesigning the original cover design for this edition, you took the old and turn it to new. Welcome back! Thank you Nike Awodiji for your continuous encouragement throughout these projects. Thank you West Alexander for being there I will always appreciate you. Thank you Judy Seals for reading through the manuscript and giving me your candid opinion. You are a true blessing. Thank you Norma Sobal for the picture, you made me look good. Thank you Ana Salas Larkin for translation to Spanish, you double my productivity.

Thank you the entire leadership team and congregation of God's Family Bible Church for your prayer and support, for buying into the vision and allowing me to begin to write again. Thank you! Thank you!! Thank you!!! Please forgive me for not mentioning your individual names you are too many to mention everybody by name. You know I truly love you.

For Parents who hunger,
For Bachelors and Spinsters who thirst,
For All the Children of the World,
&
To the **HOLY GHOST**
MY GREATEST TEACHER

TABLE OF CONTENTS

Introduction............................ xi

Chapter One: The Breakthrough Must Start With You ..13

Chapter Two: Why Children? Why Parenthood?.......30

    Foolish Children
    Wise Children
    God's Intentions & Warning Signals
    Star Hunters

Chapter Three: Doors That Should Be Closed..........63

    Spiritual Cobweb
    Foundation
    Psychology
    Orientation
    Financial Background
    Home Setting
    Wrong Friends And Associations
    School Setting And Environment

Chapter Four: The Way Out 85

INTRODUCTION

One of the vital and strong pillars, which the activities on earth rest upon, is the home (marriage). Others are that of faith or religion, education, etc. The children we are concerned about today were born into homes. People were glad for their parents when they were born; if only they knew what their lives would turn out to be. But these Children have become the stench in the world today.

Many people we see in different sectors passed through **Church**, but they came from **home**. The problem or blessing a nation gets comes from the church (in the training meted out by the Church), while the problem or blessing a Church gets comes from the home.

While in Bible School around 1985, I was on the opposition side to the debate of "formal and informal education – the home is the place for proper education." I had very logical and persuasive arguments that were presented to the audience stating that the best education we get is in the School. Our best teachers are the school-teachers, etc. But I realized that the student judges gave the highest points to the side that argued that the home is the place for the best education, because their minds were already set on the FACT (they forgot that it was a debate).

Today, we have NATURALISED the devil. When he is manifesting his attitude through our children, we tend to believe that it is the growth stage. The Child, who already knows how to dish out abuses and curse words when his/her mates know how to shout "hallelujah", is becoming a **natural** devil if he/she is not checked.

Many parents have lesson teachers or private tutors for their Children. They spend a lot on that, but how many have BIBLE TEACHERS for their children? It may not be reasonable to some. It is all right to be brilliant in Physics, but it may produce a PHYSICAL devil, its okay to know Chemistry, Biology, Mathematics, and Literature, but you may be producing a CHEMICAL, BIOLOGICAL, and MATHEMATICAL DEVIL.

If you are corrupt or messed up yourself, don't bother having children, because you will only produce after your KIND. So many people are in a haste to get married and have children without understanding the role of parents in the lives of Children.

Another dangerous thing some parents do is allowing the Children to learn things on their own without parental guidance. Psychology helps us to understand that a child learns 75% of what he/she needs to know at the age of three. The child then continues to build upon that in the next growth stage. When the child understands your CARELESSNESS at that stage, you will almost scream your life out to correct the child's behavior when going wrong.

These and many more are what the author of this book is crying out to parents. Loose your children from bondage now! This book is sufficient for Christian Education in the Children Department as well as couples' fellowship or family altar. As you read this wealthy book, my prayer is that God will open your eyes of understanding to grasp what you need to excel in your personal life and in your assignment as a parent in the precious name of Lord and savior Jesus Christ.

Pastor Anu Ojo Youth Officer, CAC worldwide

CHAPTER ONE

THE BREAKTHROUGHS MUST START WITH YOU

I first wrote and published the original version of this book eighteen years ago and by God's grace, sold thousands of copies in several countries. Even though this original version was considered to be largely successful, eighteen years has come and gone and we live in a different world now. Today those years now seems like a distant past. So many things have since changed in our world and in my own personal life and ministry. I am now married to my incredible wife with three outstanding children, two boys and a girl. Becoming a parent has afforded me an opportunity

Past trauma always creates present drama; your drama today has a direct link to your trauma yesterday, even if you can't see it yet.

to see things from the other side, from a different angle, a different perspective I never had before. I have grown as a parent and as a Christian; my walk in Christ has deepened and my point of view has expanded. As I write this enhanced edition of the book, I am not just writing from spiritual and ministerial experience, but also from physical and day-to-day personal experiences. I am now in the trenches as a parent and already fought some good fights with battle scars to prove it. I understand the euphoria and excitement of parenthood, but I also understand the challenges, fear, frustration, uncertainty and anxiety of parenting. That's why, with all humility and a renewed sense of urgency, I challenge you to allow God to speak to you through the pages of this book, please allow God to illuminate your heart and give you uncommon insights into your life and that of your family, because in that you will probably find answers to many of your life's questions.

One of the purposes of this book is to help you address things that need to be addressed in your foundation (if there is), so that you can begin to live the life you are created to live.

The title of this book is "Parents Loose Your Children From Bondage!" however, for you, it might be best called "Parent Loose YOURSELF from Bondage!" or better still "Parent Loose YOURSELF and Your CHILDREN from Bondage!" Please keep an open mind and God will speak to you. God will use this book to change your life if you will allow it.

My prayer is that the eyes of your understanding will be enlightened in Jesus' name!

Luke 6: 39-45 (ESV) *He also told them a parable: "Can a blind man lead a blind man? Will they not both fall into a pit? A disciple is not above his teacher, but everyone when he is fully trained will be like his teacher. Why do you see the speck that is in your brother's eye, but do not notice the log that is in your own eye? How can you say to your brother, 'Brother, let me take out the speck that is in your eye,' when you yourself do not see the log that is in your own eye? You hypocrite, first take the log out of your own eye, and then you will see clearly to take out the speck that is in your brother's eye. "For no good tree bears bad fruit, nor again does a bad tree bear good fruit, for each tree is known by its own fruit. For figs are not gathered from thorn bushes, nor are grapes picked from a bramble bush. The good person out of the good treasure of his heart produces good, and the evil person out of his evil treasure produces evil..."*

James 3:11-12 *doth a fountain send forth at the same place sweet water and bitter? Can the fig tree, my brethren, bear olive berries? Either a vine, figs? So can no fountain both yield salt water and fresh.*

If you are familiar with air travel, one of the in flight directions during take off is that in the case of loss of cabin pressure an oxygen mask will drop from the top of the plane. Your instructions are to first strap the mask across your own nose for easy breathing before you do the same with your child. This instruction is counter intuitive for most parents. Our instinct is to help the child first at our own expense. Yet it's a life safety sequence for both child and parent because if you don't have oxygen, you can't give oxygen. You can only give life when you've got life. What if all you have around you is death, damage and destructions? What if all you have are misfortunes, dysfunctions, disruptions and drama? What do you think you are passing to your offspring? Or what do you think you will be able to give to them?

Parents are often the key to their children's future because we reproduce after our own kind. Your parents hold the answer to many of your life's questions. They may not even realize it themselves, but have you ever notice yourself acting or talking like your parent? Have you ever wonder why certain things occurred in your life as it occurred in their lives and that of your siblings? Have you noticed similar tendencies in you as in either of your parents? If yes is the answer to any of these questions, you need to know it is not just all biological or genetics; it is more so spiritual genetics, or what I call spiritual transfers. Your parents are coded in you just as you are coded in your own children. Your parents are the fountains from which you flow, they determined your flow; you are the fountain that determines your children's flow. You are very important to your child's destiny, just as your parents are to yours. This is why it is sometimes difficult for children, who are not familiar with their parents or know their parents, to connect the dots. Connecting the dots becomes convoluted since they cannot track their flow to their fountain and they are only left to guess or wonder, unless they know how to pray through and discern things in the spirit.

Let us examine an interesting sequence in the life of some of our most important biblical figures.

The family of our spiritual patriarch Abraham, his son Isaac and grandson Jacob presents us with a rare opportunity in which the Bible actually took time to explain the events that characterized the lives of several generation of the same family. There isn't any other family that is expounded upon in scriptures like the family of Abraham and his descendants. So this allows us to see vividly the manifestations of spiritual transfer or spiritual genetics from one generation to another. Please read on.

Genesis 16:1 (NLT) *Now Sarai, Abram's wife, had not been able to bear children for him...*

Genesis 17:15-17 (NLT) *Then God said to Abraham, "Regarding Sarai, your wife—her name will no longer be Sarai. From now on her name will be Sarah. And I will bless her and give you a son from her! Yes, I will bless her richly, and she will become the mother of many nations. Kings of nations will be among her descendants." Then Abraham bowed down to the ground, but he laughed to himself in disbelief. "How could I become a father at the age of 100?" he thought. "And how can Sarah have a baby when she is ninety years old?"*

So we see Sarah, Abraham's wife, barren, but what many do not realize is that Isaac's wife Rebekah was also barren in **Genesis 25:21 (NLT).** *Isaac pleaded with the Lord on behalf of his wife, because she was unable to have children. The Lord answered Isaac's prayer, and Rebekah became pregnant with twins.*

Then look at Jacob the son of Isaac; his wife Rachel was barren also **Genesis 30:1 (NLT).** *When Rachel saw that she wasn't having any children for Jacob, she became jealous of her sister. She pleaded with Jacob, "Give me children, or I'll die!"* **Genesis 30:22-24 (NLT)** *Then God remembered Rachel's plight and answered her prayers by enabling her to have children. She became pregnant and gave birth to a son. "God has removed my disgrace," she said. And she named him Joseph, for she said, "May the Lord add yet another son to my family."*

It is essential to see that this is neither genetics nor coincidence, but purely spiritual. As we read these scriptures, we will notice that it was not Abraham that was barren because he already had a child with Hagar in Ishmael (**Genesis 16:1-4**), neither was it Isaac that was impotent because the Bible said it was Rebekah who was unable to have children (**Genesis 25:21**), nor was it Jacob because he already had children with Leah! (**Genesis 29:31-35**) But think about it, what is the probability of Abraham, Isaac and Jacob all having wives that were barren?

Abraham broke barrenness in his wife by covenant interaction with God. Isaac broke the barrenness in his wife by praying to God and Rachel's prayers broke her own barrenness to be able to give children to Jacob.

We also saw that Abraham experienced famine in **Genesis 12:10**. *And there was a famine in the land: and Abram went down into Egypt to sojourn there; for the famine was grievous in the land.*

Isaac experienced famine in **Genesis 26:1**. *And there was a famine in the land, beside the first famine that was in the days of Abraham.*

And Jacob also experienced famine as Laban ripped him off (**Genesis 30:30**). And of course we remember the famine that led him to Egypt where he discovered his son Joseph was still alive in **Genesis 42:1-2**. *Now when Jacob saw that there was corn in Egypt, Jacob said unto his sons, Why do ye look one upon another? And he said, Behold, I have heard that there is corn in Egypt: get you down thither, and buy for us from thence; that we may live, and not die.*

The three generations experienced famine in sequence. You can practically track Jacob back to Isaac, and Isaac back to Abraham.

We can also see in **Genesis 12:11-13** that Abraham lied about his wife because he was fearful of being killed for her beauty, Isaac was also fearful of being killed for Rebekah's beauty in **Genesis 26:6-9**. The same fear, the same phobia, the same paranoia and the same rationale from one generation to another in the same family. Isn't that interesting?

Genesis 12:11-13 (ERV) *Just before they arrived in Egypt, Abram told Sarai, "Look, I know that you are a very beautiful woman. When the Egyptian men see you, they will say, 'This woman is his wife.' Then they will kill me and keep you alive because they want you. So tell them that you are my sister. Then they will be good to me because of you. In this way you will save my life.*

Genesis 26:6-9 (ERV) *So Isaac settled in Gerar. His wife Rebekah was very beautiful. The men of that place asked Isaac about Rebekah. He said, "She is my sister." He was afraid to tell them Rebekah was his wife. He was afraid the men would kill him so that they could have her. After Isaac had lived there a long time, Abimelech looked out of his window and saw Isaac and his wife enjoying one another. Abimelech called for Isaac and said, "This woman is your wife. Why did you tell us that she was your sister?" Isaac said to him, "I was afraid that you would kill me so that you could have her."*

As we get to Jacob, we saw him also being deceptive as he lied to his father claiming to be his big brother Esau. Thus he got blessed claiming to be somebody he was not, just like Abraham did in **Genesis 12:16, 20**.

Genesis 27:18-24 (ERV) *Jacob went to his father and said, "Father." His father answered, "Yes, son. Who are you? "Jacob said to his father, "I am Esau, your first son. I have done what you told me. Now sit up and eat the meat from the animals that I hunted for you. Then you can bless me." But Isaac said to his son, "How have you hunted and killed the animals so quickly?" Jacob answered, "Because the Lord your God allowed me to find the animals quickly." Then Isaac said to Jacob, "Come near to me so that I can feel you, my son. If I can feel you, I will know if you are really my son Esau." So Jacob went to Isaac his father. Isaac felt him and said, "Your voice sounds like Jacob's voice, but your arms* *are hairy like the arms of Esau." Isaac did not know it was Jacob, because his arms were hairy like Esau's. So Isaac blessed Jacob. Isaac said, "Are you really my son Esau?" Jacob answered, "Yes, I am."*

Past trauma always creates present drama; your drama today has a direct link to your trauma yesterday, even if you can't see it yet.

There are many people putting Band-Aids over deep-rooted wounds, hoping that it will heal, only to discover that the wound has gotten deeper and even infected, creating more damage.

If your childhood is wounded, your parenting philosophy will be affected regardless of how much you love your children. In other words, if Mama and Papa are messed up, it's most likely the children will be messed up also. If you were parented in a dysfunctional manner, or in a dysfunctional environment, you are likely going to parent in a dysfunctional manner even when you think you are doing right because your sense of normal is skewed. So fixing your mindset, along with emotional and spiritual quirks, is crucial.

> *If your childhood is wounded, your parenting philosophy will be affected regardless of how much you love your children.*

Your foundational and childhood traumas will show up in life in unrelated ways and unexpected places if they are not dealt with, period! But it will also show up in your children and become their drama (trauma) if you don't address it, because you can only give what you have. A fountain can only send forth either sweet or bitter water from the same place, not both simultaneously. Your fountain determines your flow.

Just like the seed determines the fruit, you have already planted the seeds that germinated into your child or children and those seeds continue to grow in them even today, long after their birth.

A parent with issues will give birth to children with issues, so address your issues because it will be very difficult for me to remove the specks in my kid's eyes if my own eyes are covered with logs.

We are the fountains from which our children flow. The root controls the fruits, though roots are often hidden and invisible; yet you are the root while your children are the fruits.

We usually declare what we want, but we reproduce who we are; we reproduce after our own kind! The best way to therefore alter a product is to first alter the production process with the producer. So the remedies must start with you as parents.

We are the fountains from which our children flow.

Our children reflect us even if we disagree with who they are or what they are turning out to be. They reflect us!

We either planted the seed in our children or we allowed the seed to be planted unknowingly. Either way, we are responsible because they came from us and God entrusted the children with us. We are responsible!!!

In **Matthew 13:24-28** *Another parable put he forth unto them, saying, The kingdom of heaven is likened unto a man which sowed good seed in his field: But while men slept, his enemy came and sowed tares among the wheat, and went his way. But when the blade was sprung up, and brought forth fruit, then appeared the tares also. So the servants of the householder came and said unto him, Sir, didst not thou sow good seed in thy field? from whence then hath it tares? He said unto them, An enemy hath done this...* The essential thing about our children is not to go to sleep on them when it comes to their destiny or the active molding of their future and character, because the world and the enemy that is out to shape them does not sleep.

The children are young and tender. Their fields are very susceptible and vulnerable. It is not good enough that we plant good seeds in their lives, but we must be very protective; actively ensuring that bad seeds are not allowed in their field. Bad seeds through friends and family, bad seeds through associations and peer pressure, bad seeds through society, bad seed through television and Internet, bad seeds through social media such as Facebook, Twitter, Snapchat and Instagram, bad seeds through wrong reading and unhealthy literature, bad seed through websites and pop culture, bad seeds through video games, music and movies. Let me share this interesting experience with you. I was once praying for one of my spiritual daughters and she started manifesting several evil spirits as we prayed. Suddenly, a particular demon screamed out in a male voice, "Leave me alone, leave me alone. She is mine, she is mine."

And, in one of the rare times I ever questioned a demon, I asked, "Who are you?"

"I am viper, I am a viper," replied the male voice.

"Why are you here?" I asked.

"To destroy, to destroy." came the reply.

"How many have you destroyed?"

"None yet, she has not allowed me."

"So what are you waiting for?"

"I am waiting for the right time," the male voice said.

Then I asked, "How did you get in?"

The reply came, "She watched a film, she watched a film."

"Which film?" I queried. And the demon mentioned the name of an Indian film I had never heard before then. Hence I heard the name of that movie for the first time from the mouth of an evil spirit.

> *We usually declare what we want, but we reproduce who we are; we reproduce after our own kind!*

"It is NAGIN (the snake girl)," the demonic spirit replied.

A demon spirit gained access into this innocent girl's life through a movie! Just think about that.

"How can that happen?" you may ask. Well, your five senses are gates into your life. We are affected and influenced by what we see. God told Abraham *whatever your eyes see, it is yours, your hand can handle. That is the eye gate.* (**Genesis 13:14-16, Habakkuk 2:2**). We are affected by what we hear. The Bible says faith to do anything comes by hearing, hearing by the word of God. Fear also comes by hearing, hearing the word of man or the enemy, because fear is faith in reverse. That is the ear gate (**Psalms 18:44, Romans 10:17**). We are affected by what we taste. We all know that sin and death entered into humanity by disobedience through the mouth, eating the forbidden fruit. That is the mouth gate (**Genesis 3:2-3, 1King 13:16-24**). We are affected by what we feel. The lady with the issue of blood touched the helm of Jesus' garment and healing virtue entered her body and healed her instantly, so it is with demonic influence, it can be transferred into somebody by touch and the Bible talked about not touching the unclean things, which makes you unclean. That is the touch gate (**Luke 8:43-44, 2Corinthian 6:17, Leviticus 22:6**). We are affected by what we smell. Have you ever-smelled good food and suddenly become hungry? Have you ever smelled something and suddenly become sick or sad or emotional? Isaac was convinced he was praying for Esau when he smelled his coat on Jacob. That is the nose gate. (**Genesis 8:21, Genesis 27:27 Philippians 4:18**).

> *We usually declare what we want, but we reproduce who we are.*

So you can see that seed can be introduced into anyone's life through any of the five senses especially into the lives of innocent, unsuspecting children. That's why we can't just let our kids eat anything, watch anything, listen to anything, or just go anywhere.

There are bad seeds everywhere! They are designed to seem innocuous yet devastating. They are designed to overwhelm us as parents and consequently gain easy access into our children. Bad seeds are usually common and readily available. They are planted through things; tools, materials, situations, circumstances or technology originally design for our benefit, but are now easily exploited to plant evil seeds in our lives and in the lives of our children.

The frustrating truth about bad seeds is that they don't always spring up immediately they are sown. The seed could lay dormant for many years until one day, seemingly from nowhere, it begins to germinate, and starts bringing forth fruits which suddenly take over the child. Then parents all of a sudden wonders where all these undesirable attitudes and behaviors coming from? The seeds were sown "while men slept" while the parents were not watching, while we were preoccupied with other "IMPORTANT" things.

When problems arise with children, it's unusual for most parents to think of spiritual origins, yet most problems starts from here. Hence, many are trying to combat spiritual battles with physical weapons. Physical remedies cannot and will not solve spiritual problems, because the spiritual is way more powerful than the physical and it does control the physical, not the other way round. We therefore need to apply spiritual solutions to spiritual challenges for ultimate results. This is the reason why many problems are, at best, only contained, not fully resolved, because they are not addressed spiritually. The source has been left untouched! As the branches and limbs are trimmed, the root just shoots out new branches; it's as simple as that!

I thank God for doctors, counselors, therapist, psychologist, psychiatrist and psychotherapist, but many of the issues these professionals are called to address are beyond their expertise and way above their pay grades. They are dealing with spiritual damages manifesting in physical symptoms, but they are by no means physical or therapeutic in any way, shape or form. This is why most of their patients can only be managed not cured. So the treatment takes forever!

This book is very important to you as an adult reader whether with children or not, because it will first help you understand yourself and then help you locate your root in order to alter your fruits if need be. It explains why certain things have happened or are happening in your life right now. Just keep reading. It will take you back to the root and help you find yourself. Then you can treat yourself by the power of God in Christ, which resides in you, for out of your belly shall flow the rivers of living waters (**John 7:38**), because the Christ in you is your hope of glory (**Colossians 1:27**).

However, this book is absolutely a must for parents for two reasons: first, if your life is filled with desirable fruits, it will be helpful to be able to consciously reproduce these fruits in your children by perpetuating and reinforcing those glorious traits in the next generation thereby helping your children escape unnecessary loopholes and life's avoidable headaches.

Secondly, if you don't like the fruits you are producing, or you don't like your life's direction as a person raising a child or children, you can actively learn how to stop these cycles or traits in your life, and change direction and avoid transferring them to your innocent children. You will thereby be saving the next generation from the pain you have had to endure because it is not too late. It is still doable. Just read on!!!

The first step in resolving an issue is to acknowledge its existence and then confront it. When you run from a problem, you take solutions farther away from that problem because you are the solution. God has created us as answers to every life issue, if we will apply ourselves. We are sons and daughters of God on earth, there are no human problems man cannot solve. We are created gods on earth according to **Psalm 82:6** and **John 10:30-36** (read the book "CREATED TO MANIFEST!!!") God has empowered and equipped us to solve every single problem if we will trust HIM and apply ourselves to HIS words and HIS leadings. The Bible showed us that God had equipped us to resolve any and every issue that life might throw at us if we are willing to confront it. And explaining to us that entire creation waits for us, sons and daughters of God, to manifest (**Romans 8:19**).

The truth in this book is very potent for every age because every adult was once a kid, and parents were once children. You are what you are today because of what you were yesterday. You are here today because of where you were yesterday. Your present is as a result of your past. You are a product of your upbringing, your environment, your associations, your relationships, your parentage and your experiences.

If you have given your life to Jesus Christ, then you have heard Christ's first command, just like Lazarus did, "Lazarus come forth" (you can insert your own name there), but have you heard the second command that says, "Loose him and let him go"?

In **John 11** we read about the story of Lazarus, the friend of Jesus, and his sisters. Four days after Lazarus died Jesus showed up to raise him up. HE went to Lazarus' tomb and commanded dead

Lazarus to come forth. Let's read this amazing story from verse thirty-nine to forty four: *Jesus said, "Take away the stone." Martha, the sister of him who was dead, said to Him, "Lord, by this time there is a stench, for he has been dead four days." Jesus said to her, "Did I not say to you that if you would believe you would see the glory of God?" Then they took away the stone from the place where the dead man was lying. And Jesus lifted up His eyes and said, "Father, I thank You that You have heard Me. And I know that You always hear Me, but because of the people who are standing by I said this, that they may believe that You sent Me." Now when He had said these things, He cried with a loud voice, "Lazarus, come forth!" And he who had died came out bound hand and foot with graveclothes, and his face was wrapped with a cloth. Jesus said to them, "Loose him, and let him go." (NKJV)*

There are many Christians who had received the call back to life, but are still wrapped up in their grave clothes. They are bound hands and feet, yet they cannot understand why they are restricted and limited. Their faces are still wrapped in spiritual napkins. They are spiritually blind, can barely see anything, as blind as a bat. They live their lives on a guessing game on a trial and error basis. I called them the "maybe or maybe not Christians". Saved, but struggling. Alive, but held back. Free from death, but entangled in life. They have been called out of the grave, but remain wrapped in where they used to be. It is time for the second command to permeate and pierce through to free them from their past, so that they can enter into their future.

Just imagine someone walking around totally wrapped in grave clothes; please tell me how fun such a life would be? Yet that is the situation of many Christians in the spiritual realm today. They are covered in grave clothes, which come with grave stench, grave dirt and grave stigma. That is why life is difficult for many. Have you received the second command? Are you loosed and let go? Do you feel free to fly and fulfill all of your dreams and potentials or do you feel inhibited?

The grave clothes might be invisible to the naked eyes, but they are very apparent in the spiritual realm. Knowing that the spiritual controls the physical, we must then strive to understand that there is nothing that takes place in our physical world without first being cleared in the spiritual world, that's why the Bible adjures us to *pray without ceasing* **1Thessalonians 5:17** because your prayer changes your spiritual trajectories. Prayer changes things in the spiritual realm!

Someone may retort back and say, but the Bible says *Therefore if any man be in Christ, he is a new creature: old things are passed away; behold, all things are become new* **(2Corinthians 5:17).**

Let us see what the writer of **2Corinthians 5:17,** Apostle Paul (the greatest of all the Apostles), had to say even as a new creature, a born again believer; *For we know that the law is spiritual, but I am carnal, sold under sin. For what I am doing, I do not understand. For what I will to do, that I do not practice; but what I hate, that I do. If, then, I do what I will not to do, I agree with the law that it is good. But now, it is no longer I who do it, but sin that dwells in me. For I know that in me (that is, in my flesh) nothing good dwells; for to will is present with me, but how to perform what is good I do not find. For the good that I will to do, I do not do; but the evil I will not to do, that I practice. Now if I do what I will not to do, it is no longer I who do it, but sin that dwells in me. I find then a law, that evil is present with me, the one who wills to do good. For I delight in the law of God according to the inward man. But I see another law in my members, warring against the law of my mind, and bringing me into captivity to the law of sin which is in my members. O wretched man that I am! Who will deliver me from this body of death? I thank God through Jesus Christ our Lord! So then, with the mind I myself serve the law of God, but with the flesh the law of sin* - **Romans 7:14-25 (NKJV).**

Apostle Paul was talking about influences that were way beyond his control, explicitly detailing how he ended up doing things he never wanted to do, just found himself doing them even as a Christian; that is the grave clothes effect. The Bible says work out your deliverance (salvation) with fear and trembling because God is working in you to will and do of HIS good pleasure **(Philippians 2:12-13)**.

The Bible says the times of ignorance the Lord winks at, not the devil **(Acts 17:30** *And the times of this ignorance God winked at; but now commandeth all men every where to repent).* The days of ignorance the devil actually capitalizes on and uses against believers to hold them bound and make their lives difficult, unbearable, miserable and ineffective. Why suffer from your past if God is willing to heal you in the present, today? It's like a rich man once poor, who still refuses to repay his hundred-dollar debt, thus allowing his past to continually tarnish his future. When you ignore your past wounds without allowing God to heal them, you give the enemy an easy target. You are only as strong as your weakest link, area or spot. There are many with guns loaded from the past, which they have now turned against their present, thereby altering their future in the process.

When you ignore your past wounds without allowing God to heal them, you give the enemy an easy target.

They have brought luggage and baggage from their past into their present. Their today's race has been weighed down by their yesterday's load. The battles that started in their childhood are now being fought feverishly in their adulthood. Until you allow God to fight for you once and for all, the battle continues. You cannot do it by yourself. *Not by might, nor by power, but by my spirit, saith the Lord of hosts* **(Zechariah 4:6)**. Let God help you! That is why God is giving you the opportunity to read this book at this very moment. You are the reason this book was written. Take advantage of it!

In **Exodus 15:3** the Bible says *The Lord is a man of war: the Lord is HIS name.* So God understands battles, HE knows how to fight whenever fighting is necessary. According to **2Samuel 22:35** and **Psalm 18:34** *HE teacheth my hands to war, so that a bow of steel is broken by mine arms.* HE will not only teach your hand to war, but according to **Psalm 144:1**, HE will also teach your fingers to fight. Our God is an expert fighter who has never lost a battle before, and will not lose now. HE will fight the battle for you and with you, if that is what is necessary for your victory. However, you must first recognize and acknowledge your situation in order to allow the correct resolution. It's the same reason doctors will first explain the diagnosis before recommending the right treatment.

Many do not understand why they are the way they are, why they think the way they think or why they do what they do. They simply stroll along life's path hoping they don't do something strange or have a weird or embarrassing reaction the next time around.

Have you ever wondered why you are just angry unexplainably or sometimes upset with people without a good reason? Many times the intensity of your anger or frustration is way beyond the situation you are confronting; it's like using a machine gun on a fly. Why are you forever skeptical? Why is it so difficult for you to trust again? Why are you scared of love? Or why do you have exaggerated reactions to attention or the lack thereof? Why are you always afraid? Why do you push off those who try to help you? Why are you never good enough in your own mind? Why are you always defensive or argumentative? Why do you always think failure? Why do you want to do right but can't? Why do you feel depressed? Why do you experience posttraumatic stress without being to war? Why do you suffer severe loneliness? Why do you always need the company of people to be happy? Why do you need others approval to feel like somebody? Why do you always need alcohol or cigarettes to calm down when you have the Holy Spirit and the word of God? Why the violent tendencies? Why are you so angry and what are you angry about anyway? Why are you confused with your sexual identity? Are you a male; are you a female; why don't you know? Why the insatiable desire to get more when you have more than enough? Why the envy? Why the jealousy? Why do you always have something to say about somebody else? Why do you find pleasure in other's misfortunes or failures? Why do other's failures make you feel better about you? Why the spending problem? Why feel empty in the midst of plenty? Why never satisfied? Why the unexplainable sadness and depression? Why don't you always finish what you started? Why quick to quit? Why always running? Why the uncontrollable lies? Why the extreme selfishness and self-centeredness? Why unexplainable insomnia? Why! Why! Why?

The truth is that many of the challenges we deal with today are simply the fruits, not the root. Many times we address the visible fruits while the causative root secretly festers. Yet the root controls the fruits, but it is unnoticed because it is buried in our past. Many of these issues started when we were children, but were never dealt with. Some even started while we were in the womb, others before we were born. They have been there for so long that we now think they are normal or who we are. The sad thing is that we have passed them to our kids.

The scares and the experiences of the past dictate your responses of today.

In every adult there is a child and in every child there is an emerging adult. They constantly intermingle and interphase back and forth with each other to create our daily experience and realities. Our childhood must therefore be addressed in order for our adulthood to be whole. The scares and the experiences of the past dictate your responses of today.

CHAPTER TWO

WHY CHILDREN? WHY PARENTHOOD?

The first verse of chapter ten of the book of Proverbs tells us that: *A wise son maketh a glad father: but a foolish son is the heaviness of his mother.*

Psalm 127: 3-5 says: *Lo, children are an heritage of the Lord: and the fruit of the womb is his reward. As arrows are in the hand of a mighty man; so are children of the youth. Happy is the man that hath his quiver full of them; they shall not be ashamed, but they shall speak with the enemies in the gate.*

It is clear from the Scriptures that Children are blessings from the Lord. **Genesis 1:28** affirm this: *And God blessed them (Adam and Eve), and God said unto them, be fruitful and multiply, and replenish the earth, and subdue it: and have dominion...* Part of our fruitfulness, multiplication and replenishment is procreation.

The Psalm quoted earlier, while confirming that children are unique, also states four major reasons why God blessed humanity with them:

1. Children are meant to be the Lord's heritage, that is an inheritance of God or the physical part of God, in our homes. In other words they are the embodiment of the almighty God in the home.
2. They are also instruments of war (arrows) in the hands of their parents and an advantage over the enemy. A good

example of this is the story of Jonathan who defeated the Philistines unknown to his father. And through him, the Lord brought victory to Israel *(1Samuel 14: 1-23)*.
3. According to **Psalm 127:4**, children are also meant to increase the boldness and confidence of their parents. You will agree that a warrior is bolder when he is fully armed.
4. They are also meant to bring joy to their parents. In fact, the Bible says that the more children, the merrier **(Psalm 127:5)**.

However, **Proverbs 10:1** reveals that there are two kinds of children: the wise son who brings gladness to his father and the foolish one who constitutes heaviness to his mother. God's plan is for the former not the latter. The foolish child is not GOD's design for any home. Children are meant to bring blessings not curses, signs and wonders not for worries and woes, fun and fulfillment not for frustration and fear. The Bible says in **Isaiah 8:18** *behold, I and the children whom the Lord hath given me are for signs and for wonders in Israel from the Lord of hosts, which dwells in mount Zion.* As we go through the word of God, twelve classifications of children start to emerge and then the Son of God HIMSELF, Christ, who embodied all the characteristics of the wise children. For the sake of clarity, each classification will be symbolized by its type in the Bible. There are five classifications of foolish children and seven classifications of wise ones and then Christ who stands alone. Wouldn't you like to identify what type of child you were when growing up or what type of children you have now? That way you can influence or effect a change, if you don't like what you see. Or better still, would you like to find out how you can enhance and help your child or children as effective parents?

Below are two sets of classifications. The first set of five, the Bible called foolish and the next set of seven, the Bible called wise.

FOOLISH CHILDREN
1. Absalom, son of David
2. Hophni and Phinehas, sons of Eli

3. Joel and Abiah, sons of Samuel
4. Rehoboam, son of Solomon
5. Sons of Sceva

ABSALOM, SON OF DAVID

It's the truth, there are indeed children like Absalom, a prince, the son of King David, privileged, intelligent, handsome, loved by their parents, but completely overtaken by greed for power and deep-seated rebellion. Such children have no loyalty to the family; they will pursue their ambition at all cost, even at the expense of their parents. Whomever they have to sacrifice to achieve their selfish goals makes no difference to them. They are self-centered, manipulative, conniving and dubious in their dealings. Right is not their standard; success at all cost is their motto regardless of who is lost in the process. They will burn bridges without giving it a second thought. They will disgrace their fathers and become a reproach to their mothers. This kind of child is willing to throw an entire community in disarray if it gets them to their selfish lust or satisfies their ungodly ambition. The Bible talked about Absalom killing his own brother in revenge while manipulating his siblings and his father in the process. He used Joab to get back to his father's good grace and then turned around to seduce the entire nation to make himself king at the expense of his father's throne. He convinced Aithophel, his father's most prolific adviser, to get on his side; he plotted a coup to overthrow his own father's government and then embarrassed his parents when he slept with king's David concubines on the king's rooftop. What a doozy of a child! Absalom is rude and extremely disrespectful. Do you have a child that has no regard for you and constantly talks back at you? Do you have a child that's only nice when he or she needs something from you? The emphasis on "ONLY" and "NEED", a child that is only pleasant when he or she looks for favor. Please read 2 Samuel chapter thirteen, fourteen and fifteen. Below is an excerpt of chapter fifteen.

2Samuel 15:1-12 *And it came to pass after this, that Absalom prepared him chariots and horses, and fifty men to run before him.*

And Absalom rose up early, and stood beside the way of the gate: and it was so, that when any man that had a controversy came to the king for judgment, then Absalom called unto him, and said, Of what city art thou? And he said, Thy servant is of one of the tribes of Israel. And Absalom said unto him, See, thy matters are good and right; but there is no man deputed of the king to hear thee. Absalom said moreover, Oh that I were made judge in the land, that every man which hath any suit or cause might come unto me, and I would do him justice! And it was so, that when any man came nigh to him to do him obeisance, he put forth his hand, and took him, and kissed him. And on this manner did Absalom to all Israel that came to the king for judgment: so Absalom stole the hearts of the men of Israel. And it came to pass after forty years, that Absalom said unto the king, I pray thee, let me go and pay my vow, which I have vowed unto the Lord, in Hebron. For thy servant vowed a vow while I abode at Geshur in Syria, saying, If the Lord shall bring me again indeed to Jerusalem, then I will serve the Lord. And the king said unto him, Go in peace. So he arose, and went to Hebron. But Absalom sent spies throughout all the tribes of Israel, saying, As soon as ye hear the sound of the trumpet, then ye shall say, Absalom reigneth in Hebron. And with Absalom went two hundred men out of Jerusalem, that were called; and they went in their simplicity, and they knew not any thing. And Absalom sent for Ahithophel the Gilonite, David's counsellor, from his city, even from Giloh, while he offered sacrifices. And the conspiracy was strong; for the people increased continually with Absalom.

HOPHNI AND PHINEHAS, SONS OF ELI

1Samuel 2:12-17 Now the sons of Eli were sons of Belial; they knew not the Lord. And the priests 'custom with the people was, that, when any man offered sacrifice, the priest's servant came, while the flesh was in seething, with a fleshhook of three teeth in his hand; And he struck it into the pan, or kettle, or caldron, or pot; all that the fleshhook brought up the priest took for himself. So they did in Shiloh unto all the Israelites that came thither. Also before they burnt the fat, the priest's servant came, and said to the man that sacrificed, Give flesh to roast for the priest; for he will not have sodden flesh of thee, but raw. And if any man said unto him, Let them not fail to burn the fat presently, and then take as much as thy soul desireth; then he would answer him, Nay; but thou shalt give it me now: and if not, I will take it by force. Wherefore the sin of the young men was very great before the Lord: for men abhorred the offering of the Lord.

We also have children like the sons of Eli the high priest. Hophni and Phinehas became priests by virtue of their birth; priest by inheritance was the tradition in those days. Called or not, if they were Levite and sons of Eli, they were made a priest. For these boys familiarity with the temple had bred contempt for God. They grew up in the temple but the temple never grew in them, so they had no respect for the things of God. No boundaries, nothing was sacred to them. They were too familiar with the church, so they probably wondered what all these worshippers were huffing and puffing about anyway? Right there in the church satan got them. They had a natural disdain for the things of God. They stayed in the church while living in the flesh. They slept with the women that came to worship God right there at the church while they also defiled God's burnt sacrifice. Holiness, Purity, Prayer, Fasting, Worship, Word, Praise, Love, Grace and Sacrifice were words they heard too often to the point of saturation. They were no longer moved by what moved others and they had become indifferent to God's command. They were willing to defile God's temple without remorse. No reverence whatsoever for the things of God. Such children constitute a disgrace to their families and will cause GOD to alter HIS glorious plans for an entire family, nation, or even a whole generation. By their actions they can cause GOD to change HIS mind and place a permanent stamp of His wrath on a lineage.

1Samuel 2:22-25 *Now Eli was very old, and heard all that his sons did unto all Israel; and how they lay with the women that assembled at the door of the tabernacle of the congregation. And he said unto them, Why do ye such things? for I hear of your evil* *dealings by all this people. Nay, my sons; for it is no good report that I hear: ye make the Lord's people to transgress. If one man sin against another, the judge shall judge him: but if a man sin against the Lord, who shall intreat for him? Notwithstanding they hearkened not unto the voice of their father, because the Lord would slay them.*

JOEL AND ABIJAH SONS OF SAMUEL

These are children privileged to be fathered by a man of great spiritual stature and intimate relationship with God. No one else heard God like Samuel did, he had his fingers on God's dial. His words never fell to the ground. His sons saw honesty and uprightness at close quarters and yet ignored it. They saw integrity at the highest level and detested it. They probably considered integrity as missed opportunities for quick wealth. Integrity was not attractive to them at all. They never understood why their father had so many opportunities to enrich himself and did not. They probably saw their father as rigid and old school. Joel and Abiah the sons of Samuel probably thought their father's special grace and relationship with God covered them irrespective of what they did. They were not willing to take responsibility for themselves, but ready to take advantage of the system and subscribed to bribes for their self-enrichment. They looked for loopholes to get rich quick. They perverted justice, abused their positions and were morally bankrupt. They saw corruption as their way to make money and amass huge wealth. It was quick, it was easy, and nobody would touch them. After all they were the sons of the great prophet Samuel. These guys had criminal minds. They refused to walk in the way that had been modeled before them by their father, but ran after personal gains at the expense of the people they were privileged to lead. For these two boys, the love of money was the root of all their evil. For them, money rules, money talks and everything has a price. Nothing is priceless. They remind me of African country leaders and Washington politicians.

Their lifestyle incited a whole nation to turn her back on GOD. Israel moved from theocracy (God rule) to autocracy (man rule and dictatorship).

1Samuel 8:1-9 (NKJV) *Now it came to pass when Samuel was old that he made his sons judges over Israel. The name of his firstborn was Joel, and the name of his second, Abijah; they were judges in Beersheba. But his sons did not walk in his ways; they turned aside after dishonest gain, took bribes, and perverted justice. Then all the elders of Israel gathered together and came to Samuel at Ramah, and said to him, "Look, you are old, and your sons do not walk in your ways. Now make us a king to judge us like all the nations." But the thing displeased Samuel when they said, "Give us a king to judge us." So Samuel prayed to the Lord. And the Lord said to Samuel, "Heed the voice of the people in all that they say to you; for they have not rejected you, but they have rejected Me, that I should not reign over them. According to all the works which they have done since the day that I brought them up out of Egypt, even to this day—with which they have forsaken Me and served other gods—so they are doing to you also. Now therefore, heed their voice. However, you shall solemnly forewarn them, and show them the behavior of the king who will reign over them.*

REHOBOAM, SON OF SOLOMON

The wisest king in Israel had the dumbest prince ever, what an irony. Rehoboam was the son of King Solomon who mortgaged his father's throne on the useless advice from friends. Every child can be influence by friends to some extent, but there are some who are particularly prone to peer pressure. Their identity is completely based on friend's or other people's opinion, absolutely no mind of their own. Rehoboam is the perfect symbol of this type of children.

Solomon handed Rehoboam a twelve-tribe kingdom. By the time Rehoboam was done, it had been drastically reduced to a two-tribe kingdom with Rehoboam himself running for his dear life. He was presented with the opportunity to rule the nation with full submission or an insurrection. The foolish boy chose insurrection to the detriment of the entire country. He gave the enemy a chance to draw Israel into idolatry. What a shame! He was a child with the sense of entitlement, but he lost out in the process.

1King 12:1-20 *And Rehoboam went to Shechem: for all Israel were come to Shechem to make him king. And it came to pass, when Jeroboam the son of Nebat, who was yet in Egypt, heard of it, (for he was fled from the presence of king Solomon, and Jeroboam dwelt in Egypt;) That they sent and called him. And Jeroboam and all the congregation of Israel came, and spake unto Rehoboam, saying, Thy father made our yoke grievous: now therefore make thou the grievous service of thy father, and his heavy yoke which he put upon us, lighter, and we will serve thee. And he said unto them, Depart yet for three days, then come again to me. And the people departed. And king Rehoboam consulted with the old men, that stood before Solomon his father while he yet lived, and said, How do ye advise that I may answer this people? And they spake unto him, saying, If thou wilt be a servant unto this people this day, and wilt serve them, and answer them, and speak good words to them, then they will be thy servants for ever. But he forsook the counsel of the old men, which they had given him, and consulted with the young men that were grown up with him, and which stood before him: And he said unto them, What counsel give ye that we may answer this people, who have spoken to me, saying, Make the yoke which thy father did put upon us lighter? And the young men that were grown up with him spake unto him, saying, Thus shalt thou speak unto this people that spake unto thee, saying, Thy father made our yoke heavy, but make thou it lighter unto us; thus shalt thou say unto them, My little finger shall be thicker than my father's loins. And now whereas my father did lade you with a heavy yoke, I will add to your yoke: my father hath chastised you with whips, but I will chastise you with scorpions. So Jeroboam and all the people came to Rehoboam the third day, as the king had appointed, saying, Come to me again the third day. And the king answered the people roughly, and forsook the old men's counsel that they gave him; And spake to them after the* *counsel of the young men, saying, My father made your yoke heavy, and I will add to your yoke: my father also chastised you with whips, but I will chastise you with scorpions. Wherefore the king hearkened not unto the people; for the cause was from the Lord, that he might perform his saying, which the Lord spake by Ahijah the Shilonite unto Jeroboam the son of Nebat. So when all Israel saw that the king hearkened not unto them, the people answered the king, saying, What portion have we in David? neither have we inheritance in the son of Jesse: to your tents, O Israel: now see to thine own house, David. So Israel departed unto their tents. But as for the children of Israel which dwelt in the cities of Judah, Rehoboam reigned over them. Then king Rehoboam sent Adoram, who was over the tribute; and all Israel stoned him with stones, that he died. Therefore king Rehoboam made speed to get him up to his chariot, to flee to Jerusalem. So Israel rebelled against the house of David unto this day. And it came to pass, when all Israel heard that Jeroboam was come again, that they sent and called him unto the congregation, and made him king over all Israel: there was none that followed the house of David, but the tribe of Judah only.*

<u>SONS OF SCEVA</u>

This is the category of children that makes mockery of the things of God. They think Christianity is a joke and call the name of Jesus in vain just for fun to see what happens. They mimic praying in understanding and ridicule praying in the spirit. They crack jokes on the work of the Holy Spirit. They are skeptics and critics. They really don't believe the Bible, they question and challenge everything. This group of children usually knows enough to be dangerous, argumentative or completely, obnoxiously ignorant. They are part of the sons of Sceva. They will try to emulate the power of God to see if it actually works. They want the results and accolades without the sacrifice. They sometimes try to talk the talk without walking the walk. For these kids there will be occasions when things will get out of control. I pray your children don't fall into this category. If they are, God has a remedy for you.

Acts 19:13-16 *Then certain of the vagabond Jews, exorcists, took upon them to call over them which had evil spirits the name of the Lord Jesus, saying, We adjure you by Jesus whom Paul preacheth. And there were seven sons of one Sceva, a Jew, and chief of the priests, which did so. And the evil spirit answered and said, Jesus I know, and Paul I know; but who are ye? And the man in whom the evil spirit was leaped on them, and overcame them, and prevailed against them, so that they fled out of that house naked and wounded*

WISE CHILDREN
1. Philip's daughters
2. Children of Issachar
3. Sons of Jonadab the Rachabite
4. David, son of Jesse
5. Samuel, the child prophet
6. Jeremiah, the weeping prophet
7. Daniel, Shedrach, Meshach, and Abednego

PHILIP'S DAUGHTERS
Acts 21:8-9 *And the next day we that were of Paul's company departed, and came unto Caesarea: and we entered into the house of Philip the evangelist, which was one of the seven; and abode with him. And the same man had four daughters, virgins, which did prophesy.*

I just thought as I read this verse that it was amazing to see that the Bible emphasized the facts that these four girls were virgins. They had kept themselves pure from sexual immorality. To them purity was an asset not a liability. We live in a world where virginity is ridiculed. Where to be sexually inactive as a single person is considered abnormal, but not in the Bible. Heaven and earth may pass away, but not a single jot of HIS word will be altered. Philip's daughters showed that cleanliness and spirituality is still in vogue with God. It is sad to actually see parents worried that their unmarried children are sexually inactive and encourage them to try some sexual escapade to see how they enjoys it. To them, that is the sign of normal adolescence. This is twisted thinking. The Bible calls it fornication and adultery and God will judge such parents for such influence if they don't repent.

CHILDREN OF ISSACHAR

1Chronicle 12:32 *And of the children of Issachar, which were men that had understanding of the times, to know what Israel ought to do; the heads of them were two hundred; and all their brethren were at their commandment*

Do you have children that are just on point? They just know when and what to do. Such children are often called children of delight. They just gladden your heart and make you smile with their instinctive "rightness"; they just seem to know where to be, what to say and what to do at the right time. Such children are in the category of children of Issachar, which are children of understanding. They are exactly the opposite of children symbolized by Rehoboam who lack understanding of the time. These children are intelligent, discrete, and smart and they know what is effective at the appropriate time. Unlike Rehoboam who do not know how to gage the time and exercise productive intuitiveness and flexibility, children of Issachar are in tune with the moment; even at a young age they are considerate and know how to maneuver their way through different seasons and situation seamlessly. They understand the time; they are children every parent will be proud of. Pray that God will make your children like the children of Issachar. They will constantly put smiles on your face.

SONS OF JONADAB THE RACHABITE

In my humble opinion this is one of the best types of children described in the entire Bible, especially if raised by God-fearing parents. These are parent's dream children. Let's read about this incredible group of kids in **Jeremiah 35:1-19** *The word which came unto Jeremiah from the Lord in the days of Jehoiakim the son of Josiah king of Judah, saying, Go unto the house of the Rechabites, and* *speak unto them, and bring them into the house of the Lord, into one of the chambers, and give them wine to drink. Then I took Jaazaniah the son of Jeremiah, the son of Habaziniah, and his brethren, and all his sons, and the whole house of the Rechabites; And I brought them into the house of the Lord, into the chamber of the sons of Hanan, the son of Igdaliah, a man of God, which was by the chamber of the princes, which was above the chamber of Maaseiah the son of Shallum, the keeper of the door: And I set before the sons of the house of the Rechabites pots full of wine, and cups, and I said unto them, Drink ye wine. But they said, We will drink no wine: for Jonadab the son of Rechab our father commanded us, saying, Ye shall drink no wine, neither ye, nor your sons for ever: Neither shall ye build house, nor sow seed, nor plant vineyard, nor have any: but all your days ye shall dwell in tents; that ye may live many days in the land where ye be strangers. Thus have we obeyed the voice of Jonadab the son of Rechab our father in all that he hath charged us, to drink no wine all our days, we, our wives, our sons, nor our daughters; Nor to build houses for us to dwell in: neither have we vineyard, nor field, nor seed: But we have dwelt in tents, and have obeyed, and done according to all that Jonadab our father commanded us. But it came to pass, when Nebuchadrezzar king of Babylon came up into the land, that we said, Come, and let us go to Jerusalem for fear of the army of the Chaldeans, and for fear of the army of the Syrians: so we dwell at Jerusalem.*

Then came the word of the Lord unto Jeremiah, saying, Thus saith the Lord of hosts, the God of Israel; Go and tell the men of Judah and the inhabitants of Jerusalem, Will ye not receive instruction to hearken to my words? Saith the Lord. The words of Jonadab the son of Rechab, that he commanded his sons not to drink wine, are performed; for unto this day they drink none, but obey their father's commandment: notwithstanding I have spoken unto you, rising early and speaking; but ye hearkened not unto me. I have sent also unto you all my servants the prophets, rising up early and sending them, saying, Return ye now every man from his evil way, and amend your doings, and go not after other gods to serve them, and ye shall dwell in the land which I have given to you and to your fathers: but ye have not inclined your ear, nor hearkened unto me. Because the sons of Jonadab the son of Rechab have performed the commandment of their father, which he commanded them; but this people hath not hearkened unto me: Therefore thus saith the Lord God of hosts, the God of Israel; Behold, I will bring upon Judah and upon all the inhabitants of Jerusalem all the evil that I have pronounced against them: because I have spoken unto them, but they have not heard; and I have called unto them, but they have not answered.

And Jeremiah said unto the house of the Rechabites, Thus saith the Lord of hosts, the God of Israel; Because ye have obeyed the commandment of Jonadab your father, and kept all his precepts, and done according unto all that he hath commanded you: Therefore thus saith the Lord of hosts, the God of Israel; Jonadab the son of Rechab shall not want a man to stand before me for ever.

These kids were well trained and they adhered effectively to their father's godly training, even in his absence. Not even a prophet of repute like Jeremiah could deceive them. No person of any kind of influence or stature could manipulate them, distract them or lure them to go against their laid down principle. No celebrity, no vogue, no latest fad, nor peer pressure is strong enough to convince them against their upbringing. They constantly hear the voice of the Spirit of God that constantly reminds them of who they are. These are children that are not moved by pop culture, but by God culture. They don't run after the shiny objects. They are steady, rooted and know who they are. These are kids that give you glorious goose bumps. Even the almighty God was so impressed with them that HE cited them as the standard of stability and obedience for the children of Israel to emulate. It is amazing to see their resolve to do the right they had been taught in the face of pressure, especially in our present day of changing values. Wouldn't it be a delight to have children you don't ever have to worry about? I pray that God will make our sons and daughters like the sons of Jonadab the Rachabite in Jesus' name.

DAVID, SON OF JESSE

David was a worshipper, very different from your average kid. His passion for God was unparalleled even as a child. While other kids were doing what kids does, David was at the backside of the desert worshipping, and killing the lion and the bear, doing exploits in obscurity. The Bible never told us of anything extraordinary or spectacular about his birth or upbringing, but we notice that he was different and separated from his brothers, willing to serve and worship alone if necessary. David did not feel the need to win everybody's approval or accolades. He seemed to be comfortable being by himself, alone in God's presence. He was comfortable to grow and do exploits in private until God brought him into the public eyes. He was fearless and knew how to cease the moment. While others were running away from Goliath, he ran toward the giant and made a splash for God.

He was a special child. A giant killer, who knew how to wait for his time. David was first exposed to himself (in the wilderness as he killed a lion and a bear **1Samuel 17:34-37**), then his family (as Samuel anointed him in front of them **1Samuel 16:1-13**), then his king (as he played musical instrument for Saul **1Samuel 16:23**), then the entire nation (as he killed Goliath **1Samuel 17:45-53**). Then he waited another thirteen years from the time he was anointed king to the time he ascended the throne. His passion was just to please God. He was never late, but he was never in hurry either. I believe this is one of the things that made David special. He always followed God's timetable. Even when he had the opportunity to kill King Saul to get the throne sooner, he refused; he waited for God's time (**1Samuel 24:1-22**). He was truly a man after God's own heart. Always on God's schedule, never moved by chance or opportunity, he was always checking with God. His greatest desire was to please God.

Acts 13:22 *And when he had removed him, he raised up unto them David to be their king; to whom also he gave their testimony, and said, I have found David the son of Jesse, a man after mine own heart, which shall fulfil all my will.*

SAMUEL, SON OF HANNAH

Samuel was a covenant child pledged to God before birth, and got quickly donated and dedicated to God as soon as he was weaned in fulfillment of his mother's pledge.

1Samuel 1:21-28 *And the man Elkanah, and all his house, went up to offer unto the Lord the yearly sacrifice, and his vow. 22 But Hannah went not up; for she said unto her husband, I will not go up until the child be weaned, and then I will bring him, that he may appear before the Lord, and there abide for ever. 23 And Elkanah her husband said unto her, Do what seemeth thee good; tarry until thou have weaned him; only the Lord establish his word. So the woman abode, and gave her son suck until she weaned him. 24 And when she had weaned him, she took him up with her, with three bullocks, and one ephah of flour, and a bottle of wine, and brought him unto the house of the Lord in Shiloh: and the child was young. 25 And they slew a bullock, and brought the child to Eli. 26 And she said, Oh my lord, as thy soul liveth, my lord, I am the woman that stood by thee here, praying unto the Lord. 27 For this child I prayed; and the Lord hath given me my petition which I asked of him: 28 Therefore also I have lent him to the Lord; as long as he liveth he shall be lent to the Lord. And he worshipped the Lord there.*

So Samuel's experience integrity first hand as his mother showed him what it meant to keep one's word to the Lord, in the real sense of it. Samuel's life was therefore rooted in integrity, his mother showed him how. Samuel did not just grow in the church, he grew in God's presence, unlike Hophni and Phinehas who grew in church but were still referred to as sons of Belial (children of the devil). Instead in **1Samuel 2:26** we read; *And the child Samuel grew on, and was in favour both with the Lord, and also with men.* He was a boy that was highly favored by everyone: well-mannered, well-behaved and well beloved. He developed one of the best reputations in all of Israel from childhood on. Integrity and honesty was his hallmark, the Bible says his words never fell to the ground and no one could impeach his character. Do you know any child with such a reputation?

Samuel heard God like nobody else. God trusted him and confided in him with great secrets and he became the first prophet in Israel (**1Samuel 3:1-11**). Today we pray that God will make our children like Samuel and give us hearing ears just like that of Samuel in Jesus' name.

JEREMIAH, THE WEEPING PROPHET

Jeremiah was the prophet ordained from the womb. As a child he got overwhelmed by the gravity of his assignment and wanted a way out. These are children whose divine call is evident from birth and sometimes overwhelms them. The hand of God is evident on them even in their childhood and for this reason, many things will come against them to discourage them. Parents of such kids need to be particularly observant and careful to protect and support these incredible children. They will cry a lot not because of emotional or chemical imbalance, but because of the weight of their assignment just like Jeremiah, which many times they will not fully understand.

Jeremiah 1:4-10 *Then the word of the Lord came unto me, saying, Before I formed thee in the belly I knew thee; and before thou camest forth out of the womb I sanctified thee, and I ordained thee a prophet unto the nations. Then said I, Ah, Lord God! behold, I cannot speak: for I am a child. But the Lord said unto me, Say not, I am a child: for thou shalt go to all that I shall send thee, and whatsoever I command thee thou shalt speak. Be not afraid of their faces: for I am with thee to deliver thee, saith the Lord. Then the Lord put forth his hand, and touched my mouth. And the Lord said unto me, Behold, I have put my words in thy mouth. See, I have this day set thee over the nations and over the kingdoms, to root out, and to pull down, and to destroy, and to throw down, to build, and to plant.*

Listen to Jeremiah here as he expressed himself to God and complained about the predicament of his assignment in **Jeremiah 20:7-9** *O Lord, thou hast deceived me, and I was deceived; thou art* *stronger than I, and hast prevailed: I am in derision daily, every one mocketh me. For since I spake, I cried out, I cried violence and spoil; because the word of the Lord was made a reproach unto me, and a derision, daily. Then I said, I will not make mention of him, nor speak any more in his name. But his word was in mine heart as a burning fire shut up in my bones, and I was weary with forbearing, and I could not stay.*

DANIEL, SHEDRACH, MESHACH, AND ABEDNEGO

These types of children are those who know their God and will always be in a position to stand out from the rest and do exploits. These are children of convictions. They are not led by circumstances. They have been taught well. They will not compromise nor bow before any form of man made idol or graven image. Be it idol of food, wealth, flesh, fame, money or materialism even if it costs them dearly. For these types of children, some things are not negotiable. They have standards that set them apart from other children.

Daniel 1:8-15 But Daniel purposed in his heart that he would not defile himself with the portion of the king's meat, nor with the wine which he drank: therefore he requested of the prince of the eunuchs that he might not defile himself. Now God had brought Daniel into favour and tender love with the prince of the eunuchs. And the prince of the eunuchs said unto Daniel, I fear my lord the king, who hath appointed your meat and your drink: for why should he see your faces worse liking than the children which are of your sort? Then shall ye make me endanger my head to the king. Then said Daniel to Melzar, whom the prince of the eunuchs had set over Daniel, Hananiah, Mishael, and Azariah, Prove thy servants, I beseech thee, ten days; and let them give us pulse to eat, and water to drink. Then let our countenances be looked upon before thee, and the countenance of the children that eat of the portion of the king's meat: and as thou seest, deal with thy servants. So he consented to them in this matter, and proved them ten days. And at the end of ten days their countenances appeared fairer and fatter in flesh than all the children which did eat the portion of the king's meat.

These are the four Hebrew boys. They are the type of children that will refuse to defile themselves with the world around them. Their absence from home did neither destroy nor alter their convictions. They were in the world, but refused to be part of the world. They were in slavery, but refused to be bound to the idolatry mindset of the world they found themselves. They stayed true to their faith and put their God to the test in a foreign land and HE came through for them big time. God must be so proud of this type of children because they are the practical demonstration of **1John 2:15-29** *Love not the world, neither the things that are in the world. If any man love the world, the love of the Father is not in him. For all that is in the world, the lust of the flesh, and the lust of the eyes, and the pride of life, is not of the Father, but is of the world. And the world passeth away, and the lust thereof: but he that doeth the will of God abideth for ever. Little children, it is the last time: and as ye have heard that antichrist shall come, even now are there many antichrists; whereby we know that it is the last time. They went out from us, but they were not of us; for if they had been of us, they would no doubt have continued with us: but they went out, that they might be made manifest that they were not all of us. But ye have an unction from the Holy One, and ye know all things. I have not written unto you because ye know not the truth, but because ye know it, and that no lie is of the truth. Who is a liar but he that denieth that Jesus is the Christ? He is antichrist, that denieth the Father and the Son. Whosoever denieth the Son, the same hath not the Father:(but) he that acknowledgeth the Son hath the Father also. Let that therefore abide in you, which ye have heard from the beginning. If that which ye have heard from the beginning shall remain in you, ye also shall continue in the Son, and in the Father. And this is the promise that he hath promised us, even eternal life. These things have I written unto you concerning them that seduce you. But the anointing which ye have received of him abideth in you, and ye need not that any man teach you:but as the* *same anointing teacheth you of all things, and is truth, and is no lie, and even as it hath taught you, ye shall abide in him. And now, little children, abide in him; that, when he shall appear, we may have confidence, and not be ashamed before him at his coming. If ye know that he is righteous, ye know that every one that doeth righteousness is born of him.*

These types of children have inner fortitude, not seduced by their surrounding. They were in Babylon but did not allow Babylon into their lives. How many times have you seen kids moved to a new environment and suddenly changed with the environment? How about kids going to college and coming back to renounce everything they believed before college?

JESUS, THE SON OF THE LIVING GOD

The ultimate of all children is Christ HIMSELF who walked in perfect obedience to the father's command. There is no child that can be quite compared to HIM, but in HIM we find all the categories of the seven wise children. In HIM we found Samuel, David, Sons of Issachar, sons of Jonadab, Jeremiah, Daniel, Shedrach, Meschach and Abednego, and we find the daughters of Philip.

HE was a promised child destined for great work. HE was mysterious at times and spoke beyond HIS parent's comprehension at other times. HE was subjected to HIS parent's authority while fulfilling HIS heavenly father's vision. There were many things HIS parents do not fully understand about HIM, but they respected who HE was so they kept many things in their heart as they watched HIM grow. HE grew in wisdom, in stature, and in favor toward God and toward men. HE was not contentious as HE was growing up, but kept a low profile until HIS appointed time. This is one of the reasons HIS siblings did not believe HE was the messiah because HE was no different growing up from any other child except for few flashes of astounding knowledge like HE displayed at the age of twelve in the temple.

Luke 2:46-52 *And it came to pass, that after three days they found him in the temple, sitting in the midst of the doctors, both* *hearing them, and asking them questions. And all that heard him were astonished at his understanding and answers. And when they saw him, they were amazed: and his mother said unto him, Son, why hast thou thus dealt with us? behold, thy father and I have sought thee sorrowing. And he said unto them, How is it that ye sought me? wist ye not that I must be about my Father's business? And they understood not the saying which he spake unto them. And he went down with them, and came to Nazareth, and was subject unto them: but his mother kept all these sayings in her heart. And Jesus increased in wisdom and stature, and in favour with God and man.*

It is beneficial that parents take advantage of these classifications to identify themselves and their children. It is also possible that a child has traits from more than one category. These traits didn't just develop overnight; they started in their lives from an early stage. So parents can begin to observe their children and respond accordingly as some of these characteristics surface. It always starts when the child is young and it is much easier to deal with an acorn than an oak tree. An oak tree is an acorn that was allowed to thrive. The habit and character you allow to thrive in your children is what defines them as they grow up. The habit and character that was allowed in you is what defines you today.

> *The habit and character you allow to thrive in your children is what defines them as they grow up. The habit and character that was allowed in you is what defines you today.*

So the question is what sort of children do you have? Are they close in behavior to any of the twelve categories mentioned above? Be truthful to yourself, can they be called wise children who bring you gladness or foolish children that give you heartburn?

Well, whichever category they fall into, GOD has good news for you. By the time you are through with this book and the following outlined practical steps, bad situations will become good, the good ones will become better in Jesus' name, and GOD will be glorified in your life and that of your children in Jesus' name.

I would like you to take these three prayer points aggressively before you proceed:

1. Oh Lord, I claim every message you have for me in this book; none shall escape me in Jesus' name.
2. Every evil mechanism fashioned to hinder the work of the Holy Ghost through this book in my home, in my life, be shattered into pieces in Jesus' name.
3. I shall not study this book in vain in Jesus' name. It shall bring me outstanding results in Jesus' name.

GOD'S INTENTION & WARNING SIGNALS

GOD wants marriages to produce children like Samuel, David, and Issachar.

In **1Samuel 2:21** the Bible says, *Samuel grew up before the Lord*. I ask you, before who and what are your children growing up? Can you confidently say before the Lord? Are you setting the right example for your kids to follow?

Is God a priority in your home? Is prayer important in your home? Is the word of God emphasized in your home?

Maybe your children are growing up before violent movies and games where destructive and violent behaviors are reinforced on a regular basis. Maybe they are growing up before lustful suggestive TV shows where they are recruited into the school of immorality at a very early age. Is your house profanity laden? Is conflict a common occurrence in your vicinity? Are there positive role models in your home for your children to follow? Are you setting a godly example for them to emulate?

The enemy thrives when we pretend that he is not working while he is.

Remember the India movie (Nagin) I mentioned earlier? I later learned that the movie was very popular, especially among youth in those days back in that part of the world. How many of such movies are common in our world today? We have completely desensitized ourselves from spiritual realities pretending as if they don't exist. The unfortunate truth about this situation is that the enemy thrives when we pretend that he is not working while he is. He actually prefers to work in the dark, that's why he is called the ruler of the darkness of this world (**Ephesian 6:12**), satan rules in darkness. The more we ignore him in this area with our children, the more he grows his wings and expands his tentacles and gains territories in their lives. In other words, this is not one of those situations where ignoring satan is good. Our kids are innocent and naïve, we are responsible to protect them and redirect them on to the right course because we are the parents and are supposed to know better. The challenge is that many parents don't.

There are many books our children are reading today and many movies and games they are watching and playing today that are simply polluting their soul, corrupting their spirit while inflaming their flesh. Internet and technology have given unrestricted access into our children's lives without parental consent and we pretend as if its not so. Social media has taken over their lives dictating and molding them into the image of the world. We become what we behold, good or bad. As we behold HIS image, we are changed from glory to glory *But we all, with open face beholding as in a glass the glory of the Lord, are changed into the same image from glory to glory, even as by the Spirit of the Lord* (**2Corinthians 3:18**). So, the image that is constantly in front of our kids shapes them. We are in the end times and demons are hiding in plain sight and we don't even see them anymore. Our world has naturalized evil and we call them normal. This generation is so familiar with evil that we don't even see them anymore.

> *We are in the end times and demons are hiding in plain sight and we don't even see them anymore. Our world has naturalized evil and we call them normal.*

So the question remains, before who and what are your children growing up? It is essential to understand that what they look at, what they focus on, they become! It is better to face the question squarely now than to wait to be confronted with the same question on the Day of Judgment before the throne of the father, because we will. Remember, children are GOD's heritage, they are not yours. You are only a caretaker and one day, the rightful owner will appear, and you shall give account.

As parents, how well you bring up your children will be rewarded here on earth, as stated in **Proverbs 29:17** *Correct thy son, and he shall give thee rest; yea, he shall give delight unto thy soul.*

You will also be rewarded in heaven as a steward entrusted with the great responsibility of taking care of GOD's heritage on earth. It is either you pass or you fail.

I once saw a memorial card printed in remembrance of a late child. Some of the words I read there reflect deep spiritual facts. Here is an extract from the card:

GOD'S LENT CHILD-
I lend you for a little while.
A child of mine, GOD says.
For you to love and take care of.
She will bring her charms to gladden you.
And since there are lessons taught below.
I want this child to learn.
I've looked the whole world over In search for teachers true;
And from the things that crowd life's lane I have chosen you.
Will you give all your love? And not think the labor vain?

These are words for sober reflections.

1Samuel 2:26 says: *And the child Samuel grew on and was in favor both with the Lord, and also with men.*

Is there any trace of your children growing up in favor with GOD and men? Or is it the opposite? Do people complain regularly about your children? Are you concerned? Do you regularly receive negative reports from school? Are there regular occurrences of self-inflicted wounds? Do they cut themselves? Are they hyper aggressive?

Do they suffer from unusual bouts of depression? Are there nagging issues you just can't shake off? Does your child steal? Does he take delight in inflicting injury on others? Does he or she always meddle with dangerous abusive materials or substances? Is he or she very restless? Is he or she a constant source of worry, fear or anxiety to you? Is your child particularly disrespectful? Is he or she easily swayed by the easy instead of the right? Does your child always find the easy way out? Is your child unusually manipulative? Do you trust your child? Is your child helpful, considerate and compassionate? Does your child stick with his or her little convictions? Does your child follow instructions? Is he or she attracted to things of God or repelled by it? Is your child pro-church or anti-church? Remember David said *I was glad when they said unto me, Let us go into the house of the Lord (Psalm 122:1)*. Does church excite him or depress him? *Joshua said as for me and my house we will serve the Lord* **(Joshua 24:15)**. Is your child teachable? Is your child more likely to be stingy or generous? Is your child more likely to be compassionate or callous? Is there any continuous unexplainable sickness with your child or children?

It may even be that since the child came into the family, you noticed a series of inexplicable problems that were not there before. Has the entrance of the child into the family introduced new tension and frustration instead of joy and excitement?

Remember parents are divinely endowed with legitimate paternal and maternal instinct that sends out coded signals when things are wrong, so don't just ignore your parental compass or gyroscope. It is preferable that you address these issues and find out that they are nothing, than to ignore them and find out in the future that you missed something important, which you could have fixed at an early age.

Dearly beloved, these are just a few of the warning signals. If any of these signs have been noticed in any of your children, quick action needs to be taken.

At this point, I must mention that no parent can be completely exonerated or blameless, if the children do not turn out to be what they ought to be. It is not enough for any parent to claim, "But I tried my best." GOD has given parents enough strength and spiritual authority to train their children and mold them into what GOD wants them to be.

Proverbs 22:6 affirms this fact: *Train up a child in the way he should go; and when he is old he will not depart from it.*

GOD is serious about this point and that is why it is firmly embedded in the Scriptures. For a child to be wayward, rebellious, or termed as not so good, can only be as a result of any of the following three reasons.

First, it is possible that parents did not give the child the complete syllabus of God's training course for children. For instance, most parents strive to give their children the best education that is available, but they do not couple it with training the child in the ways of the Lord. These two dimensions of education, spiritual and physical or academic, are complementary and indispensable and as such one cannot be substituted for the other. A doctorate degree certificate cannot resist or overcome demonic influences or canal tendencies. In fact, a well educated child, who is not schooled in the things of GOD, will grow up to be a more clever devil.

A second possibility is that the parents started the training process too late. By this I mean at a time when the child's character or mannerism had already been formed.

Proverbs 19:18 says; *Chasten thy son while there is hope, and let not thy soul spare for his crying.*

This verse implies that there is a time frame involved in bringing up a child, beyond which remolding becomes very, very difficult. But do not be discouraged if you have defaulted in this area, there is still a way out, just read on.

Thirdly, there are situations where the child has been brought up in the way of the Lord, and at the right time too. But he or she still started manifesting negative traits as growth progressed. You may ask, "Why?" The answer is found in *Ephesians 6:10-18 Finally my brethren be strong in the Lord and in the power of His might. Put on the whole armour of GOD, that you may be able to stand against the wiles of the devil. For we wrestle not against flesh and blood,*

but against principalities, against powers, against spiritual wickedness in high places. Wherefore, take unto you the whole armour of GOD, that you may be able to withstand in the evil day, and having done all to stand. Stand therefore...
Praying always with all prayers and supplication in the spirit and watching thereunto with all perseverance and supplication for all saints (including your children).

Many children in these last days are neither bad nor evil; they are not directly responsible for what they turn out to be. A lot of them are under heavy spiritual bombardment from the powers of darkness. A lot are being demonically remote-controlled influenced in ways they can't control.

"Why?" You may ask. At least three reasons stand out clearly.

First, the Bible specifically states that in the end-time *iniquity shall abound, the love of many shall wax cold* (**Matthew 24:12**). This simply means that there will be an upsurge in evil and satanic activities in the last days, and we are already in the last days.

Second, there is an important fact that we have to learn about satan: he does not fight when there is nothing worth contending for. If satan sees that your child is a special one, if he sees that your child is destined for greatness, or that he or she has GOD's calling upon his or her life, then he attacks in order to forestall GOD's plan for the child. Parents, please note this point. If any of your children are always under any kind of attack, physically, spiritually, academically, or even health-wise, it is very likely that there is something very special about that child that the enemy is trying to stop. Therefore, you must be ready to help this child and fight on his or her behalf instead of always being frustrated.

Devils are trained not to fight useless battles. Every time they fight, they have seen something worth fighting for, and they are trying to see if they can win. You can call satan any name, but not a dunce. He has been with GOD before, and has a level of understanding. In fact, the Bible says in **2Corinthians 2:11** *Lest satan should get an advantage of us: for we are not ignorant of his devices,* which means he has his own deluded ways of doing things (devices). The

Bible also says, *Now, the serpent was more subtle than any other beast of the field which the Lord GOD had made...* **(Genesis 3:1)**. These verses show that the devil is not only tricky, and trickish but also diabolical and he does not waste time or energy; at least that he had learned from GOD while he was still with HIM.

Third, **I John 2:12-14** says: *I write unto you, little children, <u>because your sins are forgiven you for his name's sake.</u> I write unto you, Fathers, because you have known him that is from the beginning. I write unto you, <u>young men, because you have overcome the wicked one.</u> I write unto you, <u>little children, because you have known the Father.</u> I have written unto you, Fathers, because you have known him that is from the beginning. I have written unto you, <u>young men, because you are strong, and the word of GOD abideth in you, and you have overcome the wicked one.</u>*

The underlined portions of these Scriptures show that the strength of the church in the last days is reposed in children and youth. Their sins are forgiven, they are strong; GOD's words abide in them and they have overcome the wicked one.

Buttressing this fact, **Proverbs 20:29** says: *The glory of young men is their strength...*

The enemy therefore knows that one of the best strategies to pull down the Church and society and stop end time exploits for the Lord is to attack children and our youth. He attacks them in a variety of ways, through any means necessary. He will bully them physically and spiritually, he will use the Internet to confuse and corrupt their mind and inundate them with destructive ideas and suggestions. In these last days, it is absolutely possible for a child to not step out of the house and yet be influenced and controlled from afar through technology, laptops, games and computers. This is part of the enemy's adaptations to our present world. While the parents are behind the curve, the enemy is far advanced. These are all aimed at derailing them before they assume their roles as end-time power house, world changers, prophets, visionaries and innovators as stated in **Acts 2:17-18** *And it shall come to pass in the last days, saith GOD, I will pour out of my spirit upon all flesh; and your sons* *and your daughters shall prophesy, and your young men shall see visions, your old men shall dream dreams. And on my servants and on my handmaids I will pour out in those days of my spirit; and they shall prophesy.*

Hence, in order to destroy GOD's plans for our children, satan has commissioned specially trained commando demons against children in these last days. They are everywhere; so everywhere that we are beginning to see them as harmless. We tend to think that common means normal or harmless. We have to realize that because something is prevalent does not mean it is positive or acceptable. These demons are trained to ignore empty spiritual threats, trained to ignore warning without spiritual action, trained to ignore shedding of tears and self pity, trained to ignore medical sciences, trained to ignore rehabilitation homes and psychological therapy, trained to ignore speaking in tongues without fire, trained to ignore material comfort, which is expected to give the children contentment in order to make them good and responsible. They are trained to ignore incarceration. Their goal is to inflict maximum damage in the shortest time possible.

These forces of darkness are sent against children to wage relentless attacks for distraction and destruction. Parents who meet the twin-criteria of teaching their children in the way of the Lord and teaching them early enough, but fail to pray for them without ceasing, may still suffer loss (*1Thessalonians 5:17*).

STAR HUNTERS

In the gospel of *Matthew 2:1-12 Now after Jesus was born in Bethlehem of Judea in the days of Herod the king, behold, wise men from the East came to Jerusalem, saying, "Where is He who has been born King of the Jews? For we have seen His star in the East and have come to worship Him." When Herod the king heard this, he was troubled, and all Jerusalem with him. And when he had gathered all the chief priests and scribes of the people together, he inquired of them where the Christ was to be born. So they said to him, "In Bethlehem of Judea, for thus it is written by the prophet:*

'But you, Bethlehem, in the land of Judah, Are not the least among the rulers of Judah; For out of you shall come a Ruler Who will shepherd My people Israel.'"
Then Herod, when he had secretly called the wise men, determined from them what time the star appeared. And he sent them to Bethlehem and said, "Go and search carefully for the young Child, and when you have found Him, bring back word to me, that I may come and worship Him also." When they heard the king, they departed; and behold, the star which they had seen in the East went before them, till it came and stood over where the young Child was. When they saw the star, they rejoiced with exceedingly great joy. And when they had come into the house, they saw the young Child with Mary His mother, and fell down and worshiped Him. And when they had opened their treasures, they presented gifts to Him: gold, frankincense, and myrrh. Then, being divinely warned in a dream that they should not return to Herod, they departed for their own country another way.

We saw the story of three wise men that saw a bright star and follow that star to bless and worship the one whose star it was. In the same story we saw Herod who was threatened by the star, and hunted baby Jesus the one who the star represented for destruction. When a child's star is very bright, the enemy will hunt. There are powers of darkness that looks for bright stars for destruction; it is the spirit of Herod. This spirit is subtle, deceptive, destructive, devastating and relentlessly ruthless. It will crush anything and anyone on its way in order to try to locate and destroy the one who has the star; **Matthew 2:16 Then Herod, when he saw that he was deceived by the wise men, was exceedingly angry; and he sent forth and put to death all the male children who were in Bethlehem and in all its districts, from two years old and under, according to the time which he had determined from the wise men.** The enemy will stop at nothing in his bid to try to hunt down and destroy a child with a bright future and glorious star.

The ultimate answer is ***Wherefore take unto you the whole armour of God, that ye may be able to withstand in the evil day, and having done all, to stand. Stand therefore, having your loins girt about with truth, and having on the breastplate of righteousness (Ephesian 6:13-14)***. The answer is tireless intercession according to ***Ephesians 6:18 Praying always with all prayer and supplication in the Spirit, and watching thereunto with all perseverance and supplication for all saints*** (that includes our children).

It is essential to know that their enemy takes no breaks, no time-outs, no vacations and no casual or sabbatical leaves. They are like animals on the prowl that move around restlessly, methodically and stealthily in search of preys.

What many parents have not understood is that there is an intense battle going on between the kingdom of GOD and the devil's kingdom over our children in these last days. The two kingdoms desire the children's strength, and minds, to do divine exploits or satanic exploits. Whichever of these two kingdoms would gain control over your children is determined by your personal spiritual and physical exercises and daily routine, and involvement with these children, since you are the one with the authority over these children as their parents. You have the right and the influence to stand in the gap for them and to move them and tilt them on God's side.

> *What many parents have not understood is that there is an intense battle going on between the kingdom of GOD and the devil's kingdom over our children in these last days.*

However, many parents have not realized their roles in the lives of their children, and those who do don't know how to go about it. It is therefore no surprise that young people are the ones perpetrating some of the most egregious vices in our societies today, being caught up in drugs, rape, prostitution, abortion, armed robbery, pornography, fraud, gang related activities, school shootings, bullying, all sorts of malpractices, and immoralities, murder, suicide, occultism, and terrorism just to name a few.

Parents, you need to train, train and train your children and then pray, pray and pray again for them. Then, shall you be able to eat the fruit of your labor in the precious name of Jesus. ***Pray without ceasing (1Thessalonians 5:17).***

It is still GOD's desire that we should have children like those of Philip's the evangelist as earlier recorded in ***Acts 21:8-9***. The Bible says that Phillip had four daughters, all virgins (that is they had never been defiled) and they prophesied. Can you compare the spiritual standard of your children to those of Philip's? What about the children of Isaachar? Concerning them, the Bible records in ***1Chronicles 12:32***, that ***they had understanding of the times, to know what Israel ought to do.*** Are your children this intelligent or do you have to shout and scream your head off before they understand or do anything?

Are they as submissive and obedient as the sons of Jonadab the Rachabite who, according to the Scriptures in ***Jeremiah 35:1-19***, did not allow themselves to be deceived or confused. Not even by the prophet. Jeremiah couldn't get them to go against their father's instructions. Perhaps, your children are easily influenced and deceived with money, food and other material things. It is my firm conviction that with GOD on your side, they will be able to overcome these negative traits in Jesus' name.

Always have it at the back of your mind that your children are meant to be GOD's strong point against the devil in this end-time. They are GOD's battle-axe, God's sharp edge and weapons of war. With them, GOD will break nations in pieces and destroy kingdoms. He will also break in pieces and destroy the horses and the riders, chariots and riders, men and women, old and young, shepherd and flock, husbandman and his yoke of oxen and captains and rulers (***Jeremiah 51:20-23***). These kids got the goods!!! That's why satan wants them so bad. Don't let him get them! You have the power to stop him.

David secretly started his warfare training while tending to his father's flock as a child. (***1Samuel 17:34-37***). He had his practices with a lion and the bear that wanted to attack his father's flocks and he killed them both. He later became one of the greatest warriors ever recorded in the Bible. He was known to have never lost a single battle in his lifetime. Today, we pray that GOD should give us overcomer's anointing like that of David.

Samuel was consecrated to GOD as a child; he started hearing GOD's voice when he was a child (*1 Samuel 1:26-28; 3:1-14*). He later became one of the greatest prophets, priest and the chief judge in Israel in the Bible. He is recorded as one of the greatest prophets in history. Today, we all pray that GOD should give us hearing ears like that of Samuel.

Jeremiah complained to GOD because he was so young when the Word of GOD came to him (**Jeremiah 1:4-8**). He grew up to be one of the best intercessors in the Old Testament. He was described by many as the "weeping prophet", and wrote the books of Jeremiah and Lamentations. Today, we pray that GOD should give us the burden of intercession like he gave Jeremiah.

How about Daniel, Shadrach, Meshach and Abednego? They were trained in the way of the Lord as children. When they grew up they departed not from it. They stood on the side of GOD even in a strange land, to proclaim the statutes of the Lord and HIS ways. Through their lives of steadfastness and dedication, Jehovah was exalted and glorified in Babylon, even though that was the headquarters of idol worship in those days. Today, we pray that the GOD of Daniel, Meshach, Shadrach and Abednego should also be our GOD.

Even our Lord, our Master, our Redeemer and Savior, Jesus Christ, laid a good example. The Bible says in *Luke 2:40, 47* that as a child He *grew and waxed strong in spirit, filled with wisdom and the grace of GOD was upon Him...* At the age of twelve, he dazzled the doctors and Pharisees in the temple. The Bible says: *And all that heard him were astonished at his understanding and answers.* We also learned that He subjected Himself to His parents as they trained Him in life's lessons. He later grew up to fulfill His purpose and ministry on earth as the Redeemer and Savior of the whole wild world. Today, we pray that God will make us like our Lord and Savior Jesus Christ.

As parents, we must be alert and alive to our responsibilities of ensuring that we do not lose the battle in our home in order not to weaken the church and the society as a whole. God is counting on you, the same way He counted on Abraham. Praise God, Abraham did not disappoint HIM. Even God testified of Abraham in ***Genesis 18:19 For I know that he will command his children and household after him, and they shall keep the way of the Lord to do justice and judgement, that the Lord may bring upon Abraham that which he hath spoken of him.***

From this verse, it is very clear that by the special grace of God, we can build godly homes that honor God. If Abraham could do it, we can too. The last sentence in the verse also shows us that for God to fulfill His good plans and promises for us, we must have children and a household which thirst and pant after God.

It is also obvious from the same verse that many a times when God's plans and promises for our lives do not materialize, it may be simply because we have refused to command our children and household after God. A lot of people who run around today for deliverance and prayers would be better off if they repented of the negligence of their duties as parents, and sorted out their homes before the Lord, they would discover that many other things will simply fall into place.

My prayer, as we come to the end of this chapter, is that we shall not be ashamed of our children, in Jesus' name. I pray that God's plan for their lives will be materialized in Jesus' name!

CHAPTER THREE

DOORS THAT SHOULD BE CLOSED

I open this chapter with this all-important question, who is a challenging child? From **Proverb 10:1** we can deduce that it is a child who brings sadness to the father and heaviness to the mother. Such a child is consciously or unconsciously not fulfilling GOD's plan for his or her inclusion in that family.

However, a child may not be entirely responsible for the sorrow of his parents over him or her. It could be due to medical conditions or inherited physical or spiritual problems over which the child has no control. (Please note this point).

I would like to reassure you that the problem that Jesus cannot solve is not in existence.

In this chapter we will do some diagnoses, we will go to the source, the foundation or the root of the problems, for the Bible says *If the foundation be destroyed what can the righteous do* **(Psalm 11:3)**.

If we can identify the origin of a problem, then it is half solved. I would like to reassure you that the problem that Jesus cannot solve is not in existence. He is the Master over all situations. The master of the universe, so let's trust HIM as we go through this chapter.

The Bible gives us a clue on how to get to the root of most problems.

In **Eccl. 10:8,** we read ***Whosoever breaketh the hedge a serpent shall bite him.***

In the real world there is usually no smoke without fire. There is always a doorway, an entrance point through which the enemy comes into people's lives to wreak havoc. Once the doorway has been opened, once the hedge is broken, there is no limit to the extent that the enemy can go to inflict pain and sorrow on a person or family.

I will share some real life weird experiences with you, some of which are extreme cases.

However, the unfortunate truth about these stories is that they are more frequent than I would like to admit. The only challenge is that many people are not aware that this is what is occurring in their situation or that this is what they are dealing with. Remember ***Hosea 4:6 my people are destroyed for lack of knowledge... and Isaiah 5:13 Therefore my people are gone into captivity, because they have no knowledge: and their honourable men are famished, and their multitude dried up with thirst.***

> *Ignorance is not a virtue, it's a vice. Ignorance is not an asset, it's a liability.*

Someone once said, "What you don't know can't hurt." This statement is absolutely false and nonsensical. I would not be surprised if it was manufactured from the pit of hell. The truth is that what you don't know cannot only hurt you, but can actually kill you and destroy everything you have worked for! For the fact that someone tore up a bill or ignored the paper statement does not mean he still doesn't owe the money. Just because I ripped February off from my calendar doesn't mean the month of February does not exist.

Ignorance is not a virtue, it's a vice. Ignorance is not an asset, it's a liability. We now live in a world that pretends satan is no longer at work. We act as if the works of darkness are no longer in operation when the Bible says they are increasing. **Revelation 12:12** says ***... Woe to the inhabiters of the earth and of the sea! for the devil is come down unto you, having great wrath, because he knoweth that he hath but a short time.*** There is a reason the scriptures talk extensively about it and asked us not to ignore the devices of our enemy because if we do, satan will take advantage of us according to *2Corinthians 2:11*.That's exactly what the enemy is doing right now; taking advantage of believers because we do exactly what scriptures told us not to do. We ignore the devil's devices. So he creates new and more sophisticated ones everyday to inflict maximum damage on our children and then us.

An inconvenient truth is not any less of a truth at all! I do not advocate a dedicated focus on the devil, he doesn't deserve that much attention, but I advocate an unwavering dedicated focus on God; looking unto Jesus the author and finisher of our faith while not being ignorant of the enemy's device so that we don't become victims. The Bible admonishes us in **Ephesians 5:11** that we should reprove his work *And have no fellowship with the unfruitful works of darkness, but rather reprove them* while in the New Living Translation Bible we were told we should expose them *Take no part in the worthless deeds of evil and darkness; instead, expose them.* Pretending satan is not at work doesn't make him stop working, it actually makes him happy, and bolder, because it allows him to work unabated. As we can see from scriptures, he knows his time is short so he is working feverishly. Think about this for a second; if his time was short two thousand years ago when the book of *Revelation12:12* was written, how much shorter do you think he knows his time is now two thousand years later? That is why scriptures refer to him as the ruler of darkness of this world that means he rules in the dark (in ignorance). The less you know of his activities the more comfortable and dominant he becomes. And he has gotten so dominant lately in many people's lives, and in many families.

A while back I ministered to a young man with all sorts of psychological and emotional problems right here in Florida. He was constantly running into all kinds of trouble with the law at a very young age. His father revealed to me that the boy was exposed to all kind of sexual experiences starting at the age of ten, when his addicted mom would perform all kinds of sexual acts with different men as she made him watch and then encouraged him to go and do the same, at the age of ten! By the time he was a teenager, his mind was totally messed up, his view of life completely distorted. Several destructive doors had been opened. He was in and out of jail.

A seven-year old girl once confessed to us during prayer that she had tied up her mother's womb in the spiritual realm so that she would not be able to have a second child. She wanted to be the only child. Now think about a woman whose womb had been tied up spiritually going to a gynecologist for fertility treatments. What chance does a medical doctor have against demonic operations or demonic technology? Except the power of God intervenes, there is no amount of fertility drugs or treatments this woman could take that would help her give birth to another child.

She also said that she played the leading role (spiritually) in the theft of her father's car. A door had been opened.

Another girl told us that she tied up her mother's money in the spiritual realm to dry up her source of income, while scaring away all the people that could help the mother out of the resulting financial crisis. She also claimed to have spiritually manipulated the destiny of her two brothers. She attacked one with the spirit of insanity and the other she influenced into armed-robbery. A door had been opened.

Now think about it, how much psychiatric treatment do you think would be adequate to treat a demonically induced insanity? The doctors would probably come up with diagnosis for paranoia, bipolar disorder and schizophrenia while the criminal justice system would incarcerate the second brother continually as a repeat offender with a criminal mind. Yet these were both spiritual problems and can only be resolved spiritually.

A young girl said that she was married to a man called Frederick in the spiritual realm, and that they had seven children; five girls and two boys. She claimed to have a mansion under the sea. Now how in the world do you think this girl would be able to get married in the natural or have physical children as she grows up? There are many people that will never be able to get married physically because they are taken spiritually because the spiritual spouse will scare away any physical or natural suitors.

Have you noticed the most marriage ready people who just can't seem to find the right person? People just come and go! No one sticks or stays for no particularly good of cogent reason. Or if by any chance this person gets married, marriage is hell because the spirit spouse stirs up trouble. Just unexplainable complications and tension in the house, stupid arguments, unreasonable misbehaviors and the list goes on. Marriage counseling will not be of much help here. They need prayer!

Just like we have remote controls for many things now, there are spiritual remote controls that direct and manipulate people's destiny. Many lives are being controlled from afar, many children are being controlled from afar, many marriages are being controlled from afar, many carriers are being controlled from afar, and many spouses are being controlled from afar and the list goes on. Have you ever seen people behaving completely out of character and they can't explain why? Or have you found yourself behaving out of character and you can't explain why, just an influence came over you? If you read the book of Job chapters one and two, you will see a snippet of spiritual operations controlling physical manifestations. Everything that happened to Job was controlled from the spiritual realm. Job was now left to decide how he was going to respond, because his response would determine his final result. Based on Job's spiritual parameters in his day, he responded splendidly; he trusted God and held on to his integrity and refused to curse God and therefore came out on top, albeit, it was not easy at all, to say the least.

We as regenerated children of God; we have our own spiritual parameters in the scriptures that are designed to dictate our response and reactions to life's manifestations. That's why knowing who we are and understanding our spiritual authority and DNA is absolutely essential for a life of triumph in this dispensation.

Another child confessed, during prayer, to being responsible for the big wound that refused to heal on her father's leg. Yet he was the one taking him around in search of a solution to the problem.

A boy confessed to being responsible for his own sickness in order to waste his parent's money.

In all these cases, doors had been opened.

Sometime ago, a man came to us and complained that his 13-year old son was fond of running away from home, at times for about three weeks or more. When they eventually found him and brought him back home, he would run again for no good reason. The boy just always wanted to run away, to where and for what reason? Nobody knows. The boy didn't even understand it himself.

Other children have confessed that they deliberately failed exams in order to punish their parents. Since their failure frustrated their parents. Some children will threaten that, "If you touch me, I will faint" and truly, if you touch them, they pass out.

How about the child that is constantly angry for no known reason, children being kicked out of one school after the other, children with unexplainable violent and criminal tendencies? Have you seen kids that are just simply down right rude to their parents and, of course, everybody else? Did you manifest any of these traits while you were growing up? How about suicidal kids?

How do we explain all these weird stories?

Are these the children God ordained for homes and marriages? Definitely not! But somewhere, somehow, someway, doors were opened and the enemy gained entry into the lives of these children. Here are some ways that doors can be opened to the enemy.

SPIRITUAL COBWEB

As I have said repeatedly, events in the spiritual realm control what we experience in the physical realm. Thus, children born into an accursed family are most likely to be prone to inexplicable problems. A good example of this point in the Bible is the family of Gehazi, (*2 Kings 5:20-27*). Elisha pronounced a curse on Gehazi in verse twenty-seven *The leprosy therefore of Naaman shall cleave unto thee, and unto thy seed for ever.* Thus, it was pre-established that all the children born into Gehazi's family would be lepers no matter the generation, regardless of the medical advancement or prenatal vaccination in that generation. Such a trend would continue until the curse was broken. There is no amount of medical science, treatment or therapy that will cure such leprosy because stethoscopes cannot detect demons. It would require the breaking of the curse for such people to be cured.

Therefore some of the diseases that are considered incurable or terminal are actually spiritual. What will be more appropriate for the medical practitioners or scientist to say is that their knowledge in this particular situation has terminated.

FOUNDATION

If a builder decided to put a ten story building on a two-story foundation, we have a problem! It makes no difference how gorgeous or marble laced the outside of the building is, or how expensive the furnishing of the inside is, it is coming down. Very soon the cracks will appear and the building will eventually collapse. The foundation is not usually celebrated, or decorated, but it must be respected because it is the most important part of any house.

In **Psalm 11:3** we read that: *If the foundation be destroyed what can the righteous do?*

The foundation of the life of a child is very important. A child that is born out of wedlock needs serious prayer because the foundation of his life is faulty. I understand that this is a very common occurrence in our present society, but that doesn't change the fact that the enemy still takes advantage of such foundations. For instance, **Hosea 2:4-5** says: *And I will not have mercy upon her children, for they be the children of whoredoms. For their mother hath played the harlot. She that conceived them hath done shamefully...*

Foundational problems are particularly difficult to decipher on the surface, that's why they are called foundational problems. They are problems that are buried deep in the root of a person, which then requires history, spiritual discernment, and investigation to uncover. It is even more difficult because many times they don't begin to manifest until many years later, when every trace to the source might have been long lost.

A foundational problem often requires uncovering shameful past and embarrassing circumstances, which many are not willing to admit. There are many who would rather go down to their grave with clean reputations than admit to their dirty secrets to resolve a foundational problem.

This situation can be likened to the construction of a million dollar building on a hundred-dollar foundation. If you shortcut the foundation knowingly or unknowingly, you have already damaged the building, no matter how beautiful the building looks on the outside, the cracks will soon begin to appear on the inside, and then later on the outside. Foundation problems do not just go away! Time does not heal a foundational problem. Time makes it worse, because time makes it entrenched! The sooner a foundational problem is addressed the better! So confront yours today.

> *Foundation problems do not just go away! Time does not heal a foundational problem. Time makes it worse, because time makes it entrenched!*

An adult raped will have problems, how much more the children that result from that rape. They will definitely have foundational problem, so also are victims of child molestation.

Children of dispute will have foundational problem. This is when the father refused the pregnancy and accused the mother of adultery or cheating, or it might simply be because he doesn't want the responsibility of raising a child.

When a child is deceitfully or mistakenly passed to a different father, when a mother cannot tell who the father of a child is, foundational problems are inevitable.

When unsuccessful abortion is attempted on a pregnancy, that child will have to deal with foundational problems.

When a child bounces from foster home to foster home, foundational problems are already in place.

Adoption is great, but adopted children often experience some sense of rejection, which usually leads to foundational problems (though there may be exceptions).

Let's talk a little bit about rejection. The emotional feeling of rejection often attracts the actual spirit of rejection, which is a very devastating spirit. The assignment of this spirit is quite simple but destructive. This spirit is particularly dangerous because it is what I call a gatekeeper spirit, which simply means it is one of those spirits that open the gate of its victim's life to other bad spirits and invites them to come take residence. So this spirit for instance can open the door for suicide, homicide, anger, hatred, inferiority complex, murder, malice, loneliness, sickness, depression, phobias, addictions, suspicion, sorrow, isolation and all kinds of abuses and disorders. This is the reason a person experiencing rejection will sometimes manifest some of these other emotions. It is a gatekeeper! It mans the gate of the victim's life!

Foundational problems lead to destructive patterns, habits or behaviors. It leads to depression and unexplainable mood swings. A person suffering from foundational problems feels rejection and extreme complexes. They overreact to everything in order to compensate for their struggles. It is not uncommon for this person to often contemplate suicide, the "just end it all" syndrome. When foundational problems are in play in a child or even an adult for that matter, they will act out for no real reason and accuse the people that love them the most of not loving them at all. Foundational problems can lead to drug abuse, alcohol abuse, and sexual promiscuity. It can lead to sexual disorientation, and confusion in gender identity. It can lead to abrupt decisions, which leads to abrupt results.

When a mother considers a pregnancy as unwanted and treats the baby as such, there is likely to be foundation problems.

When a child is verbally, physically or sexually abused, then there is going to be foundational problems.

A child exposed to violence and sexual immorality at a very young age is going to suffer from foundational problems.

In addition, children who came about as a result of an incestuous relationship are likely to have foundational problems. A good example can be found in **Isaiah 16:12** *And it shall come to pass when it is seen that Moab is weary on the high place, that he shall come to his sanctuary to pray, but he shall not prevail.*

The major cause for this terrible prophesy is recorded in **Genesis 19:30-38**. From the account, we see that Lot was Moab's father and at the same time his grandfather. Also, Lot's first born was Moab's mother and sister at the same time! This odd situation arose when Lot, under the influence of alcohol, impregnated his first daughter. Moab was the product of that incestuous relationship.

Then Lot went up out of Zoar and dwelt in the mountains, and his two daughters were with him; for he was afraid to dwell in Zoar. And he and his two daughters dwelt in a cave. Now the firstborn said to the younger, "Our father is old, and there is no man on the earth to come in to us as is the custom of all the earth. Come, let us make our father drink wine, and we will lie with him, that we may preserve the lineage of our father." So they made their father drink wine that night. And the firstborn went in and lay with her father, and he did not know when she lay down or when she arose. It happened on the next day that the firstborn said to the younger, "Indeed I lay with my father last night; let us make him drink wine tonight also, and you go in and lie with him, that we may preserve the lineage of our father." Then they made their father drink wine that night also. And the younger arose and lay with him, and he did not know when she lay down or when she arose. Thus both the daughters of Lot were with child by their father. The firstborn bore a son and called his name Moab; he is the father of the Moabites to this day. And the younger, she also bore a son and called his name Ben-Ammi; he is the father of the people of Ammon to this day.

PSYCHOLOGY

Many children who feel unwanted in the family are prone to oppression, suppression, or possession by negative spirits. Some parents give the impression that children, who are neither the first nor the last-born, are not very special or important. Some parents expecting a child of a particular gender (male or female) display a level of disappointment and disdain if they don't get their preferred gender. Some children are born after their parents have had enough children and were not planning for any other child, they are usually tagged as "accident children" and the parents treat those children as such.

I would like to announce to parents that it has been clearly proven that children in the womb can hear and sense their parent's attitude toward them. Even children that are born into a family at a tense or tough period can easily "feel it in the atmosphere". Such kids usually feel uncomfortable right from the get go, from the first day in the family.

Children whose paternity was in dispute while they were in the womb, as well as children whose mothers subjected their pregnancy to abortion attempts without success, are opened to complications later in life. All the practices I have listed in this category serve to open a very dangerous gate into the lives of children through the operation of the spirit of rejection, which I wrote about earlier.

These spirits manifest in the lives of children, at different stages of development, as the children strive to fill an inexplicable internal vacuum in their lives. A vacuum that was created sometimes, even before they were born.

Some parents are excessively hard on their children; some are even out rightly wicked and abusive. The children dread them like the Israelites dreaded Egyptian taskmasters in Egypt. When a child's heart skips for fear and loses composure, when their harsh parents came along, there is a problem. It is a grand self-delusion for such parents to claim they are disciplinarian. This is not training; it is torment, torture and abuse. A good yardstick to know if you are having a positive impact on your children is to ask yourself the following questions: Do your children look forward to seeing you? Do they miss you when you are not around? Do they play with you in a relaxed atmosphere? Do you have fun together as a family?

Even in the Bible, we see that **David danced before the Lord (2 Samuel 6:14)**, and, more importantly, David said, **"Therefore will I play before the Lord" (2 Samuel 6:21)**. None of us is a better disciplinarian than God. If we can dance and play before God, then our children should be able to do the same with us. Parents, you must show love and care to the children. Give them your affectionate attention, without removing the element of discipline.

ORIENTATION

This speaks of the child's mindset. What culture? What mindset are you imbibing in your kids? Some children have been conditioned to believe that they are superior to others due to their gender, race or family background. Such children will need serious prayer and re-orientation to bring them back to earth, lest they fall after the manner of Lucifer in the Bible. Other children are conditioned to feel inferior for the same reasons. Such children will also need prayer and re-orientation to bring them to par and free them from their inhibitions. It is said that children are only born with two kinds of fears (fear of loud noise and fear of falling) every other fear is acquired.

None of us is a better disciplinarian than God. If we can dance and play before God, then our children should be able to do the same with us.

A great deal of harm is done to a child who is over-pampered and over-shielded from correction and instructions.

Proverbs 13:24 says: *Those who spare the rod of discipline hate their children. Those who love their children care enough to discipline them* (NLT).

If you don't correct your children, you don't love them. If you love them, you will be quick to discipline them (ERV).

In **Proverbs 29:15** we read: *The rod and reproof give wisdom, but a child left undisciplined brings his mother to shame* (AMP).

To discipline a child produces wisdom, but a mother is disgraced by an undisciplined child (NLT).

Therefore, no parent can claim to be too educated, or sophisticated to correct a child. To hold the opinion that it is crude and uncivilized to instruct a child simply implies you know more than the Bible, and the God of the Bible. There are explicit instructions to correct when the need arises. You would recall that in a previous chapter,

I identified the failure to give a child the full dosage of GOD's syllabus as one of the factors responsible for the waywardness of many children. One element of God's syllabus for children is the wise use of discipline, training, corrections and giving them opportunity to be responsible. This was the one singular mistake Eli made concerning his two sons (Hophni and Phinehas). When God brought the misbehavior of his sons to his attention, he basically said HE was God, let HIM do whatever HE likes. Let's read this interesting story in ***1Samuel 3:15-18 Samuel stayed in bed until morning, then got up and opened the doors of the Tabernacle[c] as usual. He was afraid to tell Eli what the Lord had said to him. But Eli called out to him, "Samuel, my son." "Here I am," Samuel replied. "What did the Lord say to you? Tell me everything. And may God strike you and even kill you if you hide anything from me!" So Samuel told Eli everything; he didn't hold anything back. "It is the Lord's will," Eli replied. "Let him do what he thinks best"*** (NLT).

You will however never understand the implications of Eli's statement until you read what God was threatening to do. Please let us see what God said HE was about to do to the house of Eli if he didn't discipline his children. ***1Samuel 3:11-14 Then the Lord said to Samuel, "I am about to do a shocking thing in Israel. I am going to carry out all my threats against Eli and his family, from beginning to end. I have warned him that judgment is coming upon his family forever, because his sons are blaspheming God and he hasn't disciplined them. So I have vowed that the sins of Eli and his sons will never be forgiven by sacrifices or offerings."*** (NLT) Isn't it amazing to see the gravity of what God planned to do against Eli because of undisciplined children and Eli told God to do whatever HE likes, because he wasn't willing to discipline his kids? What an irresponsible response from a high priest who should know better.

You would think Eli would have fallen on his face to repent and ask God for forgiveness (just like king Ahab did when he heard God's message) and then proceed promptly to bring his kids to order, but instead he was nonchalant and indifferent to something that God took so seriously. Are you nonchalant and indifferent when it comes to your children's discipline? Do you take that seriously because God does? Please remember Eli, the same God that dealt with him and his children never changes. HE is the same yesterday, today and forever (***Hebrew 13:8***). The Bible says HE doesn't change (***Malachi 3:6***).

While we are still on this topic of how to response to God's messages, I would like to show you the story of one of the worst kings in the history of Israel that I referred to earlier, Ahab. In **1King 21:17-29** *But the Lord said to Elijah, "Go down to meet King Ahab of Israel, who rules in Samaria. He will be at Naboth's vineyard in Jezreel, claiming it for himself. Give him this message: 'This is what the Lord says: Wasn't it enough that you killed Naboth? Must you rob him, too? Because you have done this, dogs will lick your blood at the very place where they licked the blood of Naboth!'"*

"So, my enemy, you have found me!" Ahab exclaimed to Elijah. "Yes," Elijah answered, "I have come because you have sold yourself to what is evil in the Lord's sight. So now the Lord says, 'I will bring disaster on you and consume you. I will destroy every one of your male descendants, slave and free alike, anywhere in Israel! I am going to destroy your family as I did the family of Jeroboam son of Nebat and the family of Baasha son of Ahijah, for you have made me very angry and have led Israel into sin.' "And regarding Jezebel, the Lord says, 'Dogs will eat Jezebel's body at the plot of land in Jezreel.' "The members of Ahab's family who die in the city will be eaten by dogs, and those who die in the field will be eaten by vultures." (No one else so completely sold himself to what was evil in the Lord's sight as Ahab did under the influence of his wife Jezebel. His worst outrage was worshiping idols just as the Amorites had done—the people whom the Lord had driven out from the land ahead of the Israelites.) But when Ahab heard this message, he tore his clothing, dressed in burlap, and fasted. He even slept in burlap and went about in deep mourning. Then

another message from the Lord came to Elijah: "Do you see how Ahab has humbled himself before me? Because he has done this, I will not do what I promised during his lifetime. It will happen to his sons; I will destroy his dynasty" (NLT)

Isn't it interesting to see one of the worst kings in all of the Bible, Ahab an idol worshipper, a murderer, the husband of one of the symbols of evil in the Bible, Jezebel, getting a reprieve from God after repentance? Yet Eli, God's high priest did not, for refusing to repent to discipline and correct his children. God takes how we bring up our children very, very seriously!

Parents! Do not leave your children to just learn for themselves, the world is filled with all sorts of unprofitable, evil, demonic information, teach them and train them. That's what the Bible recommends according to the same Bible reference above in **Proverbs 29:15** in the King James Version; *...a child left to himself bringeth his mother to shame.* Don't leave the children to themselves; get involved in their lives.

CHORES

The Bible says that Samuel was in charge of opening the windows and doors of the temple. David was in charge of tending his father's flock in the field. Even our Lord Jesus Christ was an apprentice carpenter to his earthly father, where he would have been exposed to several menial jobs and the running of errands. So parents, please encourage your children to do some life skill building chores. Teach them to be responsible and make them accountable.

Children who are shielded from a life of usefulness from an early age are being recruited into the school of nonentities.

Parents, challenge your children to gain understanding

An untrained child hardly grows up to be a force to be reckoned with, and if by a stroke of luck they attain positions of prominence, they are apt to fumble and slide back into obscurity by practice. Sometimes they will stumble and at other times they will rise to the occasion, this is all part of their growth process. Incentivize them to gain useful knowledge so that they can grow up to be useful to themselves and to society.

An untrained child hardly grows up to be a force to be reckoned with, and if by a stroke of luck they attain positions of prominence, they are apt to fumble and slide back into obscurity.

A child allowed to dictate his or her wishes at a tender age is like setting up a bomb, which might explode at an unguarded hour. Parents! Guide and instruct your children to make good choices in life. This is part of God's training curriculum for children.

FINANCIAL BACKGROUND

...Money answereth all things says **Eccl. 10:19.**

Many children can be likened to Jabez, born into sorrow and abject poverty (*1Chronicles 4:10*).

Children who are born into very poor homes are put at a disadvantage right from the start early in life. In most cases, they are deprived of an enabling environment, academically, socially and physically, that could have helped them to realize their full potential. To worsen the situation, many poor parents in an attempt to make ends meet, hardly spend enough time with the children to give them the necessary attention to help them grow up to become responsible members of society.

Thus, many children are left to their own devices, and end up in wrong company with destructive lifestyles.

On many occasions, the poverty level of a family is usually compounded by the lack of planning by the parents. When two people on minimum wages decide to have so many children, which they cannot fend for, they are deliberately inviting disaster. Such children have just been sentenced to the school of suffering and affliction. It is self-deception for such parents to blame the devil, the government or society for their predicament. This is simply self-inflicted pain.

A 14-year old once wrote us complaining about the serious financial crisis in his family. Our investigation revealed that the father, a cook, was unemployed and the mother was struggling with petty trading. Yet they had eight children to care for.

It is important that parents do not mortgage the future of their children through indiscipline, lack of wisdom, and lack of self-control. If they do, it is like issuing a check for trouble. When it is cashed, neither the parents nor society will be able to afford it.

HOME SETTING

The set-up in a family goes a long way to determine the kinds of children molded from that home because the home is where the children's characters are molded.

The epidemic of absentee fathers has devastated many children, and the prevalence of "baby mama" phenomenon is as equally destructive. When the dysfunction starts from home, there is little the society can do to rectify the situation. God created the home as the molder of the children's value; this is why the enemy works so diligently to disrupt marriages and homes.

An ungodly home inundated with strife and suspicion is far from an ideal environment to raise God-fearing children. When one or both of the parents are junkies or drunks, or perhaps it's eating disorders like bulimia or anorexia, it will surely affect the children's psyche and perception of life, because they will see life through dysfunction, which makes for a frustrating living.

When the parent or parents are erratic or unstable mentally or psychologically, then there is trouble. There is a parent that gets really angry and depressed; breaks the window, smashes the chair, kicks the dog, yells at everything and everyone and turns around to the children and sweetly says, "Honey lets go the restaurant" and acts as if nothing just happened. Well there is a problem!

In cases where the father has little or no time for the family, the mothers are left to basically single-handedly raise the children. Or, the other way around is not a wholesome or fulfilling living environment.

There are eligible men and women today who do not consider marriage because the one they witnessed between their parents was abusively disastrous. They are either dead scared of marriage or totally indifferent to it. Their spirits have been wounded!

What kind of home do you have? Do you pray in your house? Do you take time to share the word of God together? Do you eat together? Do you worship together? Do you resolve conflict quickly? Do you have godly traditions? Do you celebrate each other's success and accomplishments? Do you bear each other's burden? Do you take family events as priority? Do you sacrifice for each other? Do you support each other? Is profanity prevalent in your house? How would you describe your home setting? Is it peaceful, caring and nurturing or chaotic? Your home setting matters for the molding of your children.

WRONG FRIENDS AND ASSOCIATION

In **1Corinthians 15:33**, the Bible warns us of *Evil communications (associations) corrupt good manners.* A popular proverb says, "Show me your friend and I will tell you who you are." In **Amos 3:3**, the Bible says, *can two walk together except they agree?*

For two people to establish any friendship there must be a level of agreement or similarity between them. The similarities may be in mannerisms, background, or beliefs. And it is absolutely definite that one would influence the other. The good might influence the not so good, depending on which one is more persuasive. However, you must take note that by reason of gravity, it is always easier to drag down than to pull up.

You must be on the lookout for the types of friends your kids associate with especially when they are young and are still amenable to your guidance.

From my observation, children of similar traits are naturally drawn together.

Therefore if you don't like what you see in your child's friends, then watch out! Though it might not be that obvious now, or seems unbelievable, but your child may already be in the process of being modeled in the image of his/her friends. For in **2 Corinthians 6:14-18**, the Bible uses five strong, powerful words that link them together.

Do not be unequally yoked together with unbelievers. For what fellowship has righteousness with lawlessness? And what communion has light with darkness? And what accord has Christ with Belial? Or what part has a believer with an unbeliever? And what agreement has the temple of God with idols? For you[a] are the temple of the living God. As God has said: "I will dwell in them. And walk among them. I will be their God, And they shall be My people." Therefore "Come out from among them And be separate, says the Lord. Do not touch what is unclean, And I will receive you." "I will be a Father to you, And you shall be My sons and daughters, Says the Lord Almighty."(NKJV)

Fellowship: This means fellows in the same ship heading for the same destination. It also implies sharing together (character, beliefs, principles, aspirations, and so on).

Communion: This means bound together, stuck together, cleave together, mutual love and mutual confidence.

Accord: This implies harmony, concord.

Part: This means portion, interest, share. It also connotes what is common.

Agreement: This means consent or coming to terms with.

Now, the question is: What fellowship, communion, accord, part and agreement does your child have together with a child you describe as rebellious, troublesome, disrespectful, arrogant, worldly, ungodly or bad? Remember that it was bad friends that put Rehoboam in trouble with their wrong counsel in *1King 12:2-20*. Do you have any idea of the kind of advice and counsel your child receives from friends? If your child cannot change that bad friend, that bad friend will change your child. You therefore need to be proactive and do something fast! Don't just sit there and hope everything turns out okay! You are gaining understanding now, do something! Nothing happens if you do nothing.

The friends in your children's life are there to do any of these four things; multiply, add, divide or subtract from them. What effects are your children's friends having on their lives?

SCHOOL SETTING AND ENVIRONMENT

If you want to catch fish, you go to the water. If you want to catch a shark or a whale, you go to the sea. If you want to catch birds, you go to the sky. If you want to catch children, you go to schools. That is where you will find the greatest concentration of kids. This is why your children's schools are very important. The importance of schools cannot be overemphasized. We cannot therefore ignore what goes on in our children's school because the enemy does not. We need to continuously keep an eye on what they are teaching and imparting into our children. How many times have you seen kids come back from school with new ideas and influence? There are many good schools with staff and teachers with private agendas. Schools are also a formidable ground for peer pressure.

Some years back, one of my Christian brothers on campus approached me with the weird story of how his younger brother was initiated into witchcraft by some school friends, by simply offering him a fruit to eat.

A young girl came back home and excitedly announced to her mother, "Mummy, I can fly!" It was after a thorough interrogation that it was discovered that she had been given the spirit of witchcraft. She did not even know; she just thought flying was fun. I know we live in a world where witchcraft is glamorized with blockbuster movies breaking the box office, witchcraft costumes and witchcraft books are best sellers, but here is what God says about witchcraft:

Galatians 5:19-21 Now the works of the flesh are manifest, which are these; Adultery, fornication, uncleanness, lasciviousness, Idolatry, <u>witchcraft</u>, hatred, variance, emulations, wrath, strife, seditions, heresies, envyings, murders, drunkenness, revellings, and such like: of the which I tell you before, as I have also told you in time past, that they which do such things shall not inherit the kingdom of God.

According to Scripture, witchcraft is part of the works of the flesh and will stop a person from inheriting the kingdom of God regardless of Hollywood perspectives.

In **2Chronicles 33:1-6** especially verse six *And he caused his children to pass through the fire in the valley of the son of Hinnom: also he observed times, and used enchantments, and used witchcraft, and dealt with a familiar spirit, and with wizards: he wrought much evil in the sight of the Lord, to provoke him to anger.*

King Manasseh was another bad, bad king that ruled Israel in the days of the kings. A few of his most egregious sins included the use of witchcraft, enchantments and wizardry with familiar spirits. So we see here that witchcraft is demonic and is considered evil in the sight of God, it actually makes God extremely angry.

The Bible says in *1Samuel 15:23 For rebellion is as the sin of witchcraft, and stubbornness is as iniquity and idolatry. Because thou hast rejected the word of the Lord, he hath also rejected thee from being king.*

Parents keep your children away from witchcraft activities, books and products: it turns them against God and turns God against them.

In this third biblical reference we see that witchcraft is not just demonic or just work of the flesh, but a clear sin compared to rebellion, which leads to God's rejection.

So despite all effort to popularize witchcraft and normalize it among our children, the word of God is still unchanged as it pertains to its stand on witchcraft. It is a demonic work of the flesh and it is a rebellious sin that makes God very angry and leads to HIS express rejection.

Parents keep your children away from witchcraft activities, books and products: it turns them against God and turns God against them. It sets your children on a dangerous course for the rest of their lives. It's not worth the future headache. So help them now while you can.

To show you how serious God considers witchcraft, see what HE says in **Exodus 22:18** *Thou shalt not suffer a witch to live.*

God actually recommended the death penalty for witches in the Old Testament. Aren't you glad we are now in the New Testament with grace and better promises?

CHAPTER FOUR
THE WAY OUT

I would like parents to study this chapter with deep concentration because it contains the answers to all the questions raised in previous chapters.

In **Exodus 3:13-14,** Moses questioned GOD about His name, he asked ***Behold, when I come unto the children of Israel, and shall say unto them, the GOD of your fathers hath sent me unto you; and they shall say to me, what is His name? What shall I say unto them?" "And GOD said unto Moses I AM THAT I AM, and He said thus shall thou say unto the children of Israel, I AM hath sent me unto you."***

The name that the Almighty GOD called HIMSELF here is quite phenomenal. It explains some basic principles in Christianity. The name simply tells us that everything the enslaved Israelites needed to be free from Egypt is what GOD is. The hand of power for signs and wonders to break the backbone of Pharaoh for their release, the wind that would part the red sea for them to pass through and then close it back to drown the Egyptians, the manna in the wilderness, the water that would come out of the rock, the quail, the power to preserve their clothes and shoes to prevent them from wearing out for forty years. In other words, all they needed to get out of the land of slavery and get into the promised land of freedom is exactly what the Jehovah GOD is.

They needed no other means or smaller gods. He is sufficient and able to bring them to their expected end, even the Promised Land. GOD is still saying today that whatever you need, that is what HE will be to you. For example, if you need a miracle in your finances, that is what GOD is. Do you need healing? That is what GOD is. Do you need the power of GOD in your home, and over your children? That is what GOD is through our Lord JESUS CHRIST.

I therefore enjoin you to study this part with faith in your heart, knowing that the Bible says in **Job 14:7-9** *There is hope of a tree if it be cut down, that it will sprout again, and that the tender branch thereof wax old in the earth and the stock thereof die in the ground; yet through the scent of water it will bud and bring forth boughs like a plant.*

This passage explains that no matter how bad or hopeless the situation is, there is still great hope for you, for your children, and for your family. Just believe GOD, *with GOD, NOTHING shall be IMPOSSIBLE (Luke 1:37).*

STEP ONE
SALVATION

If you are not yet a believer, it is important for you to get born again. Without salvation, which will ignite the fire of divinity in you, the scope of your spiritual power and activities is very minimal. In fact, the Bible says that without salvation, you are an enemy of GOD (*Psalm 7:11*) and your prayers and actions in Christ are futile, abominable and unacceptable before GOD. And you cannot harness the promises of GOD because they are not for sinners (unbelievers).

Proverbs 15:6, 8, 9 says; *In the house of the righteous is much treasure: but in the revenues of the wicked is trouble. The sacrifice of the wicked is an abomination unto the Lord: but the prayer of the upright is His delight. The way of the wicked is an abomination unto the Lord: but He loved him that follow after righteousness.*

Titus 1:16 says: *They profess that they know GOD, but in works they deny Him; being abominable and disobedient, and unto every good work reprobate.*

All these Scriptures tell us the standing of a sinner before GOD. *Titus 2:14* tells us that *JESUS gave HIMSELF for us, that He might redeem us from all iniquity and purify unto HIMSELF a peculiar people zealous of good works.* So for you to be saved, you have to receive HIM who had given HIMSELF for you.

John 3:14-15 says *...Jesus is lifted up, that whosoever believeth in Him should not perish, but have eternal life.* So you have to call on HIM to save you, for *Acts 2:21* says *And it shall come to pass that whosoever shall call on the name of the Lord shall be saved.* As you confess your sins before HIM and ask HIM to save your soul, He will hear you and make you a child of GOD, a born again Christian.

STEP TWO
LOCATE THE WORD

Find out what GOD says about you, your home and your children and begin to stand on HIS word to claim and appropriate them in your life. For *good understanding giveth favour: but the way of transgressors is hard (Proverbs 13:15).* It is the "knowing" experience that will give you the needed strength to do exploits in your home and in your life. According to *Daniel 11:32 And such as do wickedly against the covenant shall be corrupted by flatteries: but the people that do know their GOD shall be strong and do exploit.*

> *Find out what GOD says about you, your home and your children and begin to stand on HIS word to claim and appropriate them in your life.*

You need to know GOD in order for you to do exploit. And *Proverbs 24:5* also says, *A wise man is strong, Yes, a man of knowledge increases strength (NKJV).* Hence knowledge will give you power.

Therefore, let us see what the Bible says about your home. *Acts 16:31 says, ...believe on the Lord Jesus Christ and thou shall be saved, and thy house* and since you have now believed, your house (your children inclusive) deserve salvation. Claim that with faith in your heart. And allow that to be settled and established in your spirit. You can also profess, confess and decree like Joshua did *"... as for me and my house, we shall serve the Lord" (Joshua 24:15).* It shall be so because the Bible says, *You shall decree a thing and it shall be established unto thee, and the light shall shine upon thy way (Job 22:28).*

Search for the Scriptures pertaining to your immediate need and work on them. By so doing, you will be setting spiritual machineries in motion to bring to pass that which you have voiced out. There is power in your mouth. That's why the Bible says *Death and life are in the power of the tongue, And those who love it will eat its fruit - Proverbs 18:21 (NKJV)*

STEP THREE
ENGAGE THE BLOOD AND THE FIRE

Exodus 12:13 And the blood shall be to you for a token upon the houses where ye are: and when I see the blood, I will pass over you, and the plague shall not be upon you to destroy you, when I smite the land of Egypt.

Revelation 12:11 And they overcame him by the blood of the Lamb, and by the word of their testimony; and they loved not their lives unto the death.

Job 1:10 Hast not thou made an hedge about him, and about his house, and about all that he hath on every side? thou hast blessed the work of his hands, and his substance is increased in the land.

Soak your home and your children in the blood of JESUS; ask the blood to wash away all your sins, the sins of your children, and those of your ancestors which might have opened doors to any bad spirits or influence affecting you or your children. Then surround yourself, your children and home with the hedge of fire of the Holy Ghost in JESUS' name.

STEP FOUR
PRAYER WARFARE SECTION

Note: This session should be prayed aloud with all seriousness and aggression (like Jacob when wrestling with the angel in *Genesis 32:24-26 And Jacob was left alone; and there wrestled a man with him until the breaking of the day. And when he saw that he prevailed not against him, he touched the hollow of his thigh; and the hollow of Jacob's thigh was out of joint, as he wrestled with him. And he said, Let me go, for the day breaketh. And he said, I will not let thee go, except thou bless me.*).

Prayer can be done with the children or the parent can use this prayer session to intercede and fight for themselves or on behalf of their children.

Thank GOD for HIS grace and mercies, for sending JESUS to die for us and enlisting us in the army of the Lord.

Thank HIM for the gift of children, for it shall be well with them.

Thank HIM for enlarging your steps under you so that your feet do not slip (***Psalm 18:36***).

Thank HIM for teaching our hands to war, and our fingers to fight spiritually (***Psalm 144:1***).

Finally, thank Him because your victory is certain in JESUS' name.

Fire of God, challenge my foundation in the name of JESUS

I stop every evil flow into my children in the name of JESUS

I challenge the foundation of my children with the fire of GOD in JESUS' name. (***Psalm 11:3***). *Remember that when the foundation is destroyed, there is trouble.*

Every Achan in the life of my children die in JESUS' name. (***Joshua 7:24-26***) *These hidden enemies, problems or evil habits that are yet to fully manifest.*

Every spirit of Absalom in the life of my children be paralyzed permanently, and loose your hold upon them in JESUS' name. (**2 Samuel 15:1-12**). *Over-ambition or ungodly ambition.*

Every spirit of Saul in the life of my children be paralyzed and loose your hold in JESUS' name (***I Samuel 13:11-14; 15:16-23; 28:15-16; Acts 9:1-5***). *The two Sauls in both the Old and New Testaments failed. New Testament Saul became Paul before he become a successful apostle.*

You powers of destiny changers, my children are not your candidates in JESUS' name. (***Isaiah 47:13***). *The astrologers, star gazers, and monthly prognosticators.*

You prince of the air, you shall have no part or portion in my children. My children are not your captives in JESUS' name. (***Ephesians 2:2***). *It rules in the life of children of disobedience.*

I reject every inspiration received from the Prince of the air in the life of my children in JESUS' name. (***Ephesians 2:2***).

Rebellious spirit, be paralyzed completely in the life of my children in JESUS' name. (***Isaiah 30:1-3, 1Samuel 15:23***). *Witchcraft is adding sin to sin.*

I come against every spirit of child destruction in the life of (mention the name of the child) in JESUS' name. (***1Samuel 2:12***). *Spirit of Belial.*

I come against every spirit of error in the life of (mention the name of the child) in JESUS' name. (***I Kings 22:22-23; 12:6-15***) *Spirit of deception and wrong counsels from unfriendly friends.*

Let every river of failure, self-destruction and sorrow flowing into the life of my children be 'dried up' from the source in JESUS' name. (***Eccl. 2:23, Proverbs 31:8***).

I bind and render to naught every power competing with GOD for my children in JESUS' name. (***Joshua 24:15***). *Joshua also made a pronouncement against them.*

I break every curse of sorrow and destruction working in the life of my children in JESUS' name. (***Galatians 3:13***). *Christ has redeemed us from the curse of the law.*

I nullify every evil covenant under which my children are operating in JESUS' name. *(For example death)* (***Isaiah 28:18***). *Every covenant outside Christ is evil.*

Over my children: I shall not build for others to inhabit, I shall not plant for others to eat; as the days of the tree are, so shall their lives be, and I shall long enjoy the works of my hands over them in JESUS' name. (***Isaiah 65:22***) *A personal decision.*

My children shall not destroy my generation in JESUS' name. (*1Samuel 2:34, 4:10-22*). *This is the prayer point priest Eli refused to pray over Hophni and Phinehas.*

O Lord, let the anointing of excellence fall upon my children in JESUS' name. (***Daniel 1:19-20***). *The four Hebrew boys operated under this anointing in Babylon.*

Establish my children, Oh Lord, as weapons of war in your hand in the name of JESUS. (***Jeremiah 51:20-23***). *The Bible says they are weapons.*

Oh Lord, establish these children as sharp arrows in my hand in JESUS' name. (***Psalm 127:4***). *Possess your possessions.*

Father Lord, let me not receive condemnation over my children on the last day in JESUS' name. (***1Samuel 2:29-36***). *Ask and you shall receive, Eli did not ask and he was condemned.*

Satan shall not inherit my children in JESUS' name (***1Samuel 2:12, Jeremiah 35:18-19; Acts 21: 8-9***). *Make up your own mind, the sons of Rachabites and Philip's four daughters could not be inherited by the devil, but he inherited those of Eli and Samuel.*

None of my children shall score points for the devil in JESUS' name. (***Acts 19:13-16***). *Seven sons of Sceva did.*

I bind and paralyze completely every strongman assigned to destroy my children in JESUS' name. (***Mark 4:27***). *You have enough power in Christ to do so.*

My children shall not contribute to the expansion of hell directly or indirectly in JESUS' name. (***Isaiah 5:14***). *The Bible says hell is still enlarging.*

Father Lord, save my children at all cost. (**Acts 16:31-33**). *A desperate prayer of heavenly-minded parents.*

Every evil gathering over my children shall fail in the name of JESUS. (***Isaiah 54:15***). *This is GOD's promise.*

My children shall be the head and not the tail in all their undertakings in JESUS' name. (***Deuteronomy 28:13***). *This is what GOD intended for them.*

My children shall constitute no sorrow to me in JESUS' name. (***Psalm 127:5***). *The Bible says that they are meant to bring Joy.*

My children shall not put me to shame in JESUS' name. (***Psalm 127:5***). *The Bible says they shall increase your boldness.*

My children shall not be for evil signs in my generation or the one to come in Jesus' name. (***1Samuel 2:34***). *Hophni and Phinehas were, in their generation.*

Every demonic wise man following my children's star for evil be blinded and paralyzed in JESUS' name. (***Matthew 2:1-2***). *As the good wise men followed JESUS' star for good, so do evil wise men follow people's stars for evil.*

Every power fighting to drown my children's glory be drowned in the pool of the blood in JESUS' name (***Rev. 12:11***).

Every evil king reigning in the lives of my children, I dethrone you in JESUS' name (***Obadiah 1:3-4***).

O Lord have no pity, do not spare, do not have mercy, but destroy every power working against my children and my marriage in JESUS' name. (***Jeremiah 13:19***).

SPECIAL ANNOUNCEMENTS

This segment of prayers is meant to be announced with boldness in our spirit and confidence in our heart as a special announcement being made by a king to his subjects with power and authority. The Bible says in ***Revelation 5:10 And (HE) hast made us unto our GOD kings and priests: and we shall reign on earth.*** Also *we read in Ecclesiastes 8:4 Where the word of a king is there is power: and who may say unto him, what doest thou.* Finally, ***Proverbs 16:10*** seals everything up, it says, *A divine sentence is in the lips of a king his mouth transgresseth not in judgment.* It simply means every proclamation you are going to make now is settled and established. Thank you, JESUS.

Right now, all spiritual channels are open to transmit your decrees to the heavens, the earth and underneath the earth, the trees will hear, the waters will hear, the rocks and all powers residing in them shall bow to the ultimate power of our Lord JESUS Christ.

Special announcement: All the children GOD has given me and those He will give me are for signs and wonders, they are for JESUS all the days of their lives in the name of JESUS (*Isaiah 8:18*).

Special announcement: Power of the spoilers, you shall not prosper over my children, you shall not spoil them, my children are not your candidates in JESUS' name. (*Judges 2:14, Jeremiah 12:12, II King 17:20, Jeremiah 51: 48, 53*). *Powers that spoil good things: career, marriages, businesses, children and so on.*

Special announcement: Power of the wasters, you shall not waste my children; my children are not your candidates in JESUS' name. (*Isaiah 54:16*). *Powers that waste opportunities, privileges, time, money, resources and lives, such that activities that should be accomplished in a few months normally could take several years.*

Special Announcement: Power of the emptier, you shall not empty my children; my children are not your captives in JESUS' name. (*Nahum 2:2*) *Powers or forces that empty people of good things, ideas, wisdom, initiatives, talents and so on.*

Special Announcement: Power of the devourers, you shall not devour my children; my children are not your prey in JESUS' name. (*Malachi 3:11*). *Powers that eat up good things, or saps a person of good virtues.*

Special announcement: As from today onwards, my children are made a spectacle unto the world, and to angels and to men, to the glory of GOD the father in JESUS' name. (*1Corinthians 4:9*). *Like Shedrack, Meschack, and Abednego in Babylon.*

Special Announcement: My Children shall reach God's goal for their lives whether the devil likes it or not in JESUS' name. (*2Timothy 4:7-8*). *Moses with all his anointing and meekness did not reach his goal, but thank GOD Paul did. Make your choice.*

Thank you God for answering my prayers, for YOU are a GOD that answers prayers (*Mark 11:24; Philippians 4:6*).

STEP FIVE
EVEN YOU CAN MINISTER DELIVERANCE (PRACTICAL SECTION)

Every parent or child affected, one way or the other, by what I have written so far is advised to go through a thorough session of prayer or deliverance ministration. It can be carried out more than once, if the occasion calls for it. Every believer, parent or parent-to-be can cast out devils. *These signs shall follow them that believe in my name. They shall cast out devil...* **(Mark 16:17)**.

Once you believe in the Lord Jesus Christ, the first sign that is supposed to be operational in your life is the ability to cast out devils.

But unfortunately, most Christians are scared of demons and deliverance ministrations. The Bible makes it clear that *GOD has given us POWER to tread upon serpent and scorpions and over all the powers of the enemy, and HE said nothing shall by any means hurt us* (**Luke 10:19**).

Therefore, in this section, every parent (or parent-to-be) will be trained or taught on how to carry out simple deliverance on themselves and on their children without any pastor, or any specially trained deliverance minister. You will be surprised, or even shocked, at what GOD can do through you. But in case there are still some fear or worries, I advise you to see a more experienced minister in this field. God bless you.

The steps listed in this section are not rigid. I am not saying you must mandatorily follow these steps or that if you don't follow them, God cannot do what He wants to do in your lives or that of your children. No, that is not the point. What I am outlining here are just some guidelines aimed at helping you to achieve an easier, and more effective, deliverance ministration.

The most important factors toward achieving a very successful ministration is the leading of the HOLY SPIRIT and the ANOINTING which breaks the yoke. The steps are as follow:

Choose a specific date that you will commit into the hands of the Lord for the ministration. Prepare for that day with fasting, prayer and Scriptures. On the chosen date, the parent who wants to carry out the deliverance is advised to fast, even if the child does not fast (though it is advisable that the child fast if the child can), but that of the parent is essential. This is usually recommended because you do not know the strength of the demon you are confronting, and our Lord JESUS made it clear that there are some demons who will never be cast out, except by fasting and prayer (*Mark 9:28-29*).

Pray for boldness, strength and courage. Ask GOD to anoint you with the authority of ease. Remember that it is not by power, nor by might, but by my SPIRIT says the Lord of hosts (*Zechariah 4:6*).

Carry out these first four steps listed earlier in this chapter.

Lay your hand on your child, then rebuke and paralyze the spirit you have noticed. Ask them firmly to go out and leave your children in JESUS' name, get out of (*mention your child's name*) in JESUS' name." Mention the spirits one after the other and pray until you are convinced that the spirit is out, then move to the next spirit. (In case of aggressive reactions or manifestation, RELAX, there is nothing to be scared of, you are a child of GOD. Pray and ask GOD to take control in JESUS' name).

I need to point out that it is not compulsory that there should be any demonic demonstration or manifestation before the demons go out. So do not be discouraged that the deliverance is unsuccessful because there is no physical violent manifestation. A very powerful demon or legions of demons can leave a person without any aggressive reaction. Demons can leave through just a drop of tears from the child's eyes, or by yawning, coughing, sneezing, belching, passing out gas, or even by breathing. Another point to note here is that evil spirits are not visible. They are spirit beings. But on some occasions, their demonic deposit in the deliverance candidates has been seen to be physically expelled. GOD allows this to happen sometimes in order for people to appreciate the extent to which HIS power has delivered them from danger and destruction. Thus, people undergoing deliverance have been known to vomit or pass out stuff.

The child should also be asked to renounce and denounce these spirits by open confessions against them, such as, "I dissociate myself from the spirit of witchcraft in JESUS' name. I no longer belong to you. I am a child of GOD; leave me alone in JESUS' name." Or the Child can say, "I rebel against you spirit of rebellion or stubbornness operating against me or through me in JESUS' name. And I break my link with you in JESUS' name." etc. If the child is a baby and is unable to make the confession, you can easily say them on his or her behalf by laying your hands on his or her head.

Ask the fire of GOD to purge the child's spirit, soul and body, from the top of his head to the soles of his feet. Do this consistently until you receive a release that the purging is thorough. Ask the blood of JESUS to wash the child clean from all demonic deposits, evil consumptions and remnants in JESUS' name. Keep at it until you are convinced that it is done.

When you are through with these preceding steps, you now move to the stage of breaking curses and evil covenants with demons such as: serpentine spirits, ancestral spirits, water spirits, witchcraft, death, infirmity, spirit husbands, spirit wives, and so on. I have to sound a gentle note of warning here that at this stage, some attention, persistence and patience are needed to dislodge the curses and covenants, especially for first-timer ministers. It is well known that the most difficult section of many deliverance ministrations is breaking of curses and covenants, because it involves an agreement between two parties. The agreement may be conscious or unconscious, direct or indirect. But here more often than not, the demons try to prove stubborn because they often believe that they have a legal ground to remain unchallenged or undisturbed. Take your time, as GOD strengthens you, you will win in JESUS' name. You can voice out something like this; "I break every curse of..." (If you know any, mention it) placed upon your life by... (Mention the spirit or person in question) by the reason of the anointing of GOD upon my life in JESUS' name.

I rebuke and cast out every spirit keeping the curse or covenant in place in JESUS' name. Pick the curses and covenants you have noticed in your child and make sure you have the assurance of accomplishment before you move on.

Pray generally, challenging hidden strangers in their lives. You may not know if they are there or not, so challenge them in JESUS' name. The Bible says in **Psalm 18:44-45, *As soon as they hear of me, they shall obey me: the strangers shall submit themselves unto me. The strangers shall fade away, and be afraid out of their close places*.** Ask their habitation in your child's life to be desolate in JESUS' name.

Cover the child with the blood of JESUS and incubate him/her in the fire of the HOLY GHOST in JESUS' name.

Decree that there shall be no reinforcement, reuniting, regrouping and re-strengthening against the child and yourself in JESUS' name. Remember the words of JESUS in ***Matthew 12:43-45, When the unclean spirit is gone out of a man, he walketh through dry places, seeking rest, and findeth none. Then he saith, I will return into my house from whence I came out and when he is come, he findeth it empty, swept and garnished. Then goeth he, and taketh with himself seven other spirits more wicked than himself, and they enter in and dwell there; and the last state of that man is worse than the first. Even so shall it be also unto this wicked generation.***

Thank GOD for answered prayers and enabling strength. Watch the child for some days and you will be surprised at what GOD has done through you.

STEP SIX: KEYS TO POSSESSING BLESSED CHILDREN
<u>PREVENTIVE, PROCTETIVE, DEFENSIVE & PRESERVATIVE MEASURES ON THE CHILDREN</u>

Train you children in the way of the Lord, teach them how to pray, and encourage them to study the Bible (don't just tell them, "Go and read your Bible.") Pick up the Bible with them and discuss it in a friendly atmosphere. If you can afford it, make the Bible exciting to them by giving them gifts to reward them for a good performance in your quiz or discussion. The gift does not have to be anything big. The most important thing is that children love a sense of competition, and they value the prizes they win. The wafers or candy you give as a result of their performance in the Bible quiz is more valuable to them than the one you give them for doing nothing.

In addition, whenever they come to you to complain about pains or discomfort, always ask them, "Have your prayed about it? You have to talk to GOD our heavenly father about it." If the child says he/she hasn't prayed, hold his/her hand and pray along with him/her, then you can take any action you deem fit to relieve the pain or discomfort. Even if you do not have faith in the prayers you said (though you should!), this attitude will gradually develop your child in the way of the Lord. After sometime, you will soon notice praying about issues and situations will naturally rub off on the child. And in this way, the child will start developing a relationship with JESUS.

Make sure that the devotions are not skipped. Encourage them to take their memory verses seriously; this will complement your efforts on the Bible Quiz. Also, try to get them involved in the children's activities in the church.

Be careful about what you say to your children. Parents have a special spiritual authority over their children, and satan is quick to take hold of what you say against your children. These two biblical verses support this position. **Proverbs 12:14 and Proverbs 13:2** say,

Make sure that the devotions are not skipped. Encourage them to take their memory verses seriously

A man shall be satisfied with good by the fruit of his mouth... And, ***A man shall eat good by the fruit of his mouth.***

Many parents, who have worked hard on their children, simply destroy all their efforts on these children with their tongue. Avoid negative pronouncements, and evil verbal verdicts. The Bible says in **Colossians 4:6** *Let your speech be always with favour, seasoned with salt, that ye may know how ye ought to answer every man.*

Negative utterances have enough power to erode all that the parents have invested in their children. Thus many parents need deliverance of the tongue, the Bible says you shall be justified or condemned by what you say (***Matthew 12:37***).

Pray well concerning your children's school and pay attention to what they are being taught. This might be a bit difficult because most of the schools are polluted. But there are still a few good Christian schools around. But even if your children have to go to public schools, constantly surround your children in prayer.

Give your children enough attention. You are more than just a parent to your children, you are also their pastor, and you will give an account to God on these responsibilities. The child that is not well trained will mortgage, vandalize and destroy all the wealth and prestige his/her parents have acquired over the years. I pray that GOD will help us in this area in JESUS' name.

Watch out for the type of company your children keep, even when they are matured. Break all ungodly, unhealthy associations – even if you have to go out of your way to do this.

Be careful about where your children go. By allowing them to go just anywhere, you might be breaking the hedge around your kids. Allowing them to go to wrong places might open them up to ungodly influences.

Develop some interest in the type of films or movies your children watch. Take time to find out their favorite programs. It is often satan's device of choice to infiltrate the children with both local and foreign demons. Please watch the games they play. I have seen some video games bearing the names of actual existing demons. Watch out for this, it is another satanic end-time award winning bestseller. Pay attention to the websites they visit online. Engage parental control, block out wrong sites and control what they take in.

Control what they take in through the five senses, as you now know that those are entrance gates into their lives. A word is enough for the wise.

Lay good examples for your children to follow. A mango tree cannot bear blue berries; an orange tree cannot bear plantain. You can only produce the fruit after your own kind. Watch your own dressing, attitude, spiritual seriousness, choice of words and place of interest. Remember, the children will only want to do what they see their mommy and daddy do. Your lifestyle is the greatest teaching aid material they have. Do not tell your children to lie on your behalf, because they will soon start lying to you. Don't encourage them to be disrespectful to someone else because they will soon be disrespectful to you. Don't send them to buy alcohol, cigarettes, or condoms because they will soon begin to try them out. Children are very inquisitive and they will want to find out what you do with all they see with you. Protect their heart. It's their greatest asset.

STEP SEVEN
CONCLUSION

Always trust GOD and have faith in HIM, that ...*he which hath begun a good work in you will perform it until the day of Jesus Christ* (*Philippians 1:6*). And that *With God's power working in us, he can do much, much more than anything we can ask or think of* (*Ephesians 3:20 ERV*). Give thanks to HIM; in all things HE is more than able. P-R-A-I-S-E the LORD, for HIS mercies endureth forever.

Remain Blessed and Rapturable.

ABOUT THE AUTHOR

Abolaji Muyiwa Akinbo is the Founding Pastor of God's Family Bible Church, Palm Coast, Florida, U.S.A.

A prayer warrior, bestselling author, teacher and preacher of the word with a strong desire to help people achieve their dreams and fulfill their God given potential.

He is a graduate of University of Lagos, Nigeria, Rhema Bible Training College Broken Arrow Oklahoma, and Life Christian University Tampa. His friends and congregation fondly calls him Pastor Bo.

He is married to Doranda Akinbo who pastors with him in Florida. They are blessed with three incredible children, two boys and a girl; Ore, Ayo, and Sade.

Find Abolaji Muyiwa Akinbo (Pastor Bo) online at:
Abolajiakinbo@gmail.com
PLCBbook.com
Abolajiakinbo.com
Muyiwaakinbo.com
AkinboInternationalminitries.com
Facebook.com/muyiwa.akinbo

Abolaji Muyiwa Akinbo
P. O. Box 350655
Palm Coast, Fl 32135